EQUALITY

EQUALITY

ROBERT L. CARTER

DOROTHY KENYON

PETER MARCUSE

LOREN MILLER

With a Foreword by

CHARLES ABRAMS

Pantheon Books

A Division of Random House

New York

CONTENTS

The Quota System

CHARLES ABRAMS

The year 1965 is seeing the racial issue snarled in conflicts between one right and another. The right to dwell where one chooses is pitted against the right to dwell with whom one chooses. Equality under law is confronted by the claim that the long subordination of the Negro's rights demands preferential treatment, which in turn is attacked as "discrimination in reverse." The right of a Negro child to an integrated school is confronted by the right of a white child to attend a school in his own neighborhood.

Complicating the racial issue is a jungle of verbal abstractions such as "discrimination," "segregation," "in-

Charles Abrams is a Visiting Professor at the Massachusetts Institute of Technology and has led many United Nations housing missions abroad. His most recent book is *Man's Struggle for Shelter* (M.I.T. Press, 1964).

tegration," "open occupancy," "deliberate speed," "ghettoization," and "color blindness," none of which terms have been clearly defined. Now the term "quota system" has been added to the racial jargon and it has become one of the most contentious terms in the civil rights dialectic. It has divided the ranks on the civil rights front and those who use it have even been charged with favoring discrimination.

The term "quota" had no unsavory connotation in its earlier use and simply meant a proportional part or share, such as a quota of funds or troops to be contributed by towns to a central government as their fair allotment. The term was also used in economic planning programs to control imports and exports in the national interest. It was not until 1924, when the American immigration law was passed, that it acquired its initial blemish. Reflecting the feeling of Nordic superiority and fearful that the nation's control might pass to an alien cultural group, Congress authorized what came to be known as a "quota" system, under which certain unwanted alien groups were all but barred from entering the country through a designation of a token number of eligibles. Eastern Europeans as well as Orientals were discriminated against deliberately in their right to enter the country. The contrivance was not a quota but a ban. It cleverly invoked a word which in other contexts had a respectable meaning for its unrespectable purpose. The quota law was vehemently attacked by liberals as discriminatory and was soon associated with exclusionary practices based on race, color, and national origin.

The term "quota system" then worked its way into the American educational system when Jewish students, many of them either first or second generation immigrants, were banned from medical schools without respect to their grades or qualifications. The schools would accept a token number of Jewish students and thereby avoid the charge that they were banning Jews altogether. A nation-wide survey in 1945 showed that American medical colleges were receiving 35,000–40,000 applications annually from 14,000 individuals, of whom 5000–7000 were Jews. About 6000 non-Jews were admitted each year as compared to only 500 Jewish applicants. Some of the Jewish students were forced to seek their educations in inferior universities in Europe and as far away as Africa. When applications were made by Jewish students to enter Howard University in Washington, then an all-Negro institution, one of the professors told me that the university was pressed by the nation's medical fraternity to follow the course of other medical schools and limit the number of Jewish admissions lest the Negro medical school become predominantly Jewish.

This first experience with the "quota system" in education has some lessons for us with regard to the current race question. Jews at the time were still feeling some of the strictures of American anti-Semitism—it should be recalled that racial restrictive covenants of the period often embraced Jews as well as Negroes, Syrians, and others, and it was not until the 1950s that medical colleges were opened more freely to Jewish students.

In most medical schools the use of the system was primarily to exclude Jews and, as in the case of the immigration law, it should not have been called a quota system but an interdiction. It also posed a serious problem for universities that were willing to open their doors to Jews without numerical restriction, for such an open policy would have turned the nondiscriminating college into an all-Jewish school.

Yet had all schools abolished their quotas simultaneously or liberalized them sufficiently, with the intention of eliminating the need for restrictions, the fear that Jewish students would overwhelm the schools with their numbers would have disappeared, for a large proportion matriculated in New York and there were simply not enough Jewish applicants in the whole country to do the overwhelming elsewhere. At best they would have constituted a fifth of the attendance in approved medical schools. This is just about the present proportion.

The system was not only exclusionary but unnecessary. It created the very problem it was allegedly trying to avoid, for it set up a waiting backlog of Jewish students threatening to homogenize the first institution removing its barriers. It created a case for the self-fulfilling prophecy.

As enlightenment set in and as the pressures eased, the use of "quotas" waned. But the odium which the system had inherited survived. It has worked its way into the current debate on Negro equality—in employment, in the public schools, and in housing. A few examples will point up the nature of the current quota dilemma.

A major communications agency with a nondiscriminatory employment policy found that most of the messengers applying for jobs were Negro. Because most of its local offices now had a predominant number of Negro employees, white workers were refusing to apply and those already working there were leaving. The company asked the local antidiscrimination agency whether it could limit the number of its Negro workers to one-third so that it could maintain its integrated employment policy. This would have required identification for employment on the basis of color and the rejection of Negro applicants when the tipping point was reached. This was viewed as violating the local statute and as a "quota system." The company's alternatives thereafter were either to allow its offices to become all-Negro or to violate the law by restricting its hiring so as to achieve the socially desirable goal of an integrated employment pattern. Which of the alternatives is better in the long run and what the company's legal rights should have been were never finally determined.

The situation, however, is far more troublesome in schools and housing, particularly in cities with substantial Negro populations, such as Washington, D.C., with a 54 percent Negro population; Newark, New Jersey, with a

50 percent Negro population; Detroit, with a 29 percent Negro proportion; and Baltimore, with a 30 percent Negro population. In many cities, moreover, there is intense residential segregation within particular areas. In Phoenix, Arizona, about 97 percent of the city's Negroes live within a radius of one mile of the railroad tracks or the river bed. In Newark, 83 percent are concentrated in six of Newark's twelve delineated districts. In Indianapolis, 89 percent live in one area known as Center Township.[1]

These residentially segregated patterns inevitably lead to segregation in public schools in which pupil selection made on the basis of neighborhood residence has been traditional. Such segregation has been held to be a form of discrimination. In the words of the United States Supreme Court: ". . . the policy of separating the races is usually interpreted as denoting the inferiority of the Negro group. A sense of inferiority affects the motivation of a child to learn." When such segregation has the sanction of law, it tends to retard "the educational and mental development of Negro children and to deprive them of some of the benefits they would receive in a racially integrated school system." [2] It should therefore seem a laudable purpose to prevent segregation, break it up where it exists, and employ every lawful device to achieve an integration. This, however, is easier said than

---

[1] *Report of the U.S. Commission on Civil Rights* (Washington, D.C.: U.S. Government Printing Office, 1963), p. 163.

[2] *Brown* v. *the Board of Education* (347 US 483).

done. More often it has been done without being said, and the issue has never been raised.

In the effort to achieve integration, beleaguered school officials have tried to devise numerous plans, one of the most notable of which is the so-called Princeton plan. Where two schools exist, one in a Negro and the other in a white neighborhood, one school under the plan is assigned to children from the lowest to the third grade; the other to children from the fourth to the sixth grade. Children from both sections will then attend each school. These and other plans (including zoning and gerrymandering of districts) to achieve affirmative integration have, however, raised the issue of whether they call for a quota system and whether quotas can be legally employed to create a racially balanced school population. Its proponents say that only in this way can nonsegregation be assured. Others charge that prescribing quotas limits opportunities by excluding qualified pupils who exceed the quotas prescribed. The principle once established, they argue, may become entrenched to the detriment of individual liberty.[3]

While the debate rages and other devices are being desperately sought that will satisfy everybody, the nation is seeing its central city schools becoming all Negro. It is seeing white families withdrawing their children from predominantly Negro schools, moving to all-white suburbs, or sending their children to private schools. Segrega-

[3] Jack Greenberg, *Race Relations and American Law* (New York: Columbia University Press, 1959), p. 250.

tion in public schools in Northern cities is fast becoming the established pattern and the more it becomes confirmed, the more difficult it will be to alter it.

At the base of the quota dilemma is the housing segregation prevalent in American cities and suburbs. Negro segregation is sometimes voluntary, for a tendency of minority groups has been to settle among their own people and institutions. As often it is also involuntary in that the Negro's income is about two-thirds of white income and his inability to compete for the better living areas tends to head him toward the city's slums. Added to this factor are the social strictures which compulsorily confine Negro families to segregated sections of communities by excluding them from the white urban and suburban areas.

A breakup of the segregation pattern in housing would seem to be a prerequisite for the transition to desegregation. But it is in the housing issue that much of the contention over words, principles, and policies has taken on the semblance of a Donnybrook. Efforts to open up white areas to Negroes by limiting the number of Negro tenants in a project are charged with violating the "color-blind" doctrine and setting up quota systems. On the other hand, allowing Negroes unlimited entry into a project would bring about undesirable segregation in schools as well as neighborhoods.

Near Pittsburgh, a nonprofit organization selected a site in a white suburban area in which to build an integrated project. When the white neighbors objected,

they were assured that the project would not be predominantly Negro. The sponsors thereafter proceeded
to select tenants so as to maintain a proportion of 80
percent whites and 20 percent Negroes. After a time,
however, 7 vacancies appeared and the only applicants
for these vacancies were 7 Negro families. The owner
held up the Negro applications until it could secure
more white applicants to maintain the project's balance.
It argued, among other things, that one reason for the
concentration of Negro applications in the project was
that the city had not done its job of making other private
owners accept Negroes as tenants. The argument was rejected. The local Commission on Human Relations held
the policy to be discriminatory. The owner's practices
were roundly condemned as a quota system in violation
of the local law against discrimination. Because the nonprofit agency's sponsors were prominent members of
the community, the case was never taken to court.

In New York City, both a local and a state law
provide against racial discrimination in housing and
proscribe any written or oral inquiry with regard to an
applicant's race. Because the city's housing projects were
threatened with a lasting segregated pattern, the New
York City Housing Authority in 1959 instituted what
it called a "phase program." "Phase program" is another
addition to the civil rights jargon and because it did not
have the disesteem of "quota system," the Authority be-
lieved it would have a better chance of sailing through
the troubled sea of ideological logomachy. The Authority

identified four types of projects in its extensive public-housing inventory: (*a*) those occupied predominantly by nonwhites which it thought should be "better integrated" by increasing the number of white tenants, (*b*) projects occupied predominantly by Negro and Puerto Rican families which were showing a tendency toward an imbalance and which therefore required more white and non-Puerto Rican families, (*c*) projects occupied by white tenants in which Negro and Puerto Rican applicants should receive preference, and (*d*) projects with extensive Puerto Rican occupancy which involved an effort to place Puerto Ricans into other projects. The Authority insisted it was not using a quota system in that its policy was not based on fixed percentages and that it was in fact trying to foster integration. Because the incomes of Negroes and Puerto Ricans were lower than incomes of other families, its projects were tending to become occupied predominantly by Negroes and Puerto Ricans, many more of whom qualified under the low-income limitations fixed by Federal and state housing agencies. These minority concentrations discouraged white applications, brought school segregation to the neighborhoods of the projects, as well as segregation of the playgrounds and institutional services. Worse still, the placement of a predominantly Negro-occupied project brought segregation to neighborhood schools that had been well integrated.

The New York State Commission for Human Rights, in an unsolicited opinion, called the practice a quota system—"a deliberate limitation and control of the racial proportions of tenants." This was held to violate the state law against discrimination. The Commissioner said:

If a quota were to be instituted in the fields of employment, public accommodations and education, it would be immediately branded by men of good will as repugnant. Why, therefore, should it be applied in the field of housing? Yet, such a system is advocated by many well-intentioned individuals and private agencies.[4]

"The slightest compromise with true equality of opportunity, even for worthy ends," said the Commissioner, "would open the way for the unbridled use of a quota system for restrictive and discriminatory ends." It would encourage "tokenism" and perpetuate the concept that there are racial differences which affect the person's desirability as a neighbor. A quota once established, he continued, would become part of the mores. The Commissioner's opinion ended with an ominous admonition:

Law is the expression of the will of the people and a foundation stone of the structure of democratic government. It regulates the orderly conduct of the affairs of man. Were it otherwise, chaos—even tyranny—would prevail. . . . "The end justifies the means" doctrine may not in our judicial system supplant existing relevant statutes.[5]

One important fact on which the Commissioner failed

---

[4] *Report on Informal Investigation of Tenant Selection Practices and Policies of the New York City Housing Authority,* Bernard Katzen, April 9, 1962, p. 11. For a contrary view, see *Miles* v. *N.Y.C. Housing Authority,* Feb. 9, 1959, rendered by me when I was the Commission's chairman.

[5] Katzen, *ibid.,* pp. 13, 14.

to elaborate, however, was that the law which is the "foundation stone" of democratic government also condemns segregation. In fact, the purpose of the state law against discrimination is stated as not only to "eliminate" but to "prevent segregation," [6] and the term "discriminate" under the state law also includes "to segregate or separate." [7]

If the housing authority was trying in good faith to prevent segregation, was it intending to violate the law's true purpose or seeking in fact to observe it?

The issue is by no means simple, for it is "each individual who is entitled to the protection of the laws—not merely a group of individuals, or a body of persons according to their numbers." [8] And there is much to the argument that a project or school limited to a Negro composition of, say, 25 percent might be a workable arrangement and even fair to Negroes as a group but would nevertheless deny rights to a Negro applicant who happened to constitute the 26th percentile.

The issue is so difficult in its implications that intelligent Negro leaders have chosen to sweep it under the rug. They are loath to approve any system which challenges the Negro's rights to absolute equality, but they also recognize that unless some controls are exercised, segregation in housing, neighborhoods, and schools will be the consequence. And while some Negroes openly condemn

---

[6] State Law Against Discrimination, Section 290.
[7] Civil Rights Act, 18B.
[8] *Mitchell* v. *U.S.*, 313 US 80 (1941).

anyone favoring a quota, benign or unbenign, others hesitate to condemn the socially minded administrators who in good faith try in a difficult situation to avoid segregation in neighborhoods and schools through a practical—even if technically illegal—procedure.

The issue, however, when swept under the rug, will not stay there. Without taking a firm position on the issue, there is the danger that courts will condemn honest efforts to integrate on strictly legalistic grounds and that a body of law will be built up which will leave no room for breaking down segregated patterns, however estimable the intent.

It has been the fate of the civil rights battle that its progress has been continuously snarled by symbols and even well-intentioned reforms. Thus symbolic principles, like States' rights, local autonomy, home rule, and decentralization, have now become the means for denying the Negro equal rights in the South as well as in the suburban North. Zoning became racial zoning, and restrictive covenants racial covenants. Slum clearance, which attained high respect among liberals and minorities, has often been the device for ousting Negroes from established footholds, while publicly aided housing in Stuyvesant Town, New York, received court sanction to the deliberate exclusion of Negro families. The case of the quota system is the first in which a dishonorable symbol supplies the impetus for striking down what is often an honorable purpose.

It is in fact not unlikely that if the friends of civil

rights build up the arguments against the quota system without allowing for identification of motivations on the facts of each case, the courts of the South will find their arguments and the precedents they establish useful when sanctioning a refusal of a school board to accept a given number of Negro children. This has already been indicated by the case of a well-intentioned developer named Morris Milgram, who sought to build a development in an all-white section of Deerfield, Illinois. He proposed to sell 10 to 12 of 51 houses to Negroes. After considerable harassment by white neighbors and by local officials, Milgram brought suit to enjoin a condemnation of his property. The court held, among other things, that Milgram's "controlled occupancy" pattern was illegal and a violation of the Fifth and Fourteenth amendments.[9] Milgram's sincere effort to introduce Negroes into a white neighborhood was held to be "forced and controlled." "If there is to be controlled or forced integration," said the court, "it is most certainly a matter for action by the people through their government and not by a private corporation, which, when all is said, has as its object the motive of profit. . . ." Here motive was disregarded and, if my inferences are correct, quota systems are legal when enacted by a public agency, irrespective of its motive, but illegal when employed by a private developer, even when his intent is good. If motivation is irrelevant as a criterion, not only may we be headed for segregation and "tokenism," but we may

---

[9] 182 F. Supp. 681.

be opening the door to some dangerous judicial propositions.

How, therefore, can the conflict between the color-
blind doctrine and the honest effort to achieve integration be resolved? One way for a housing authority might
be to:

1. Select more open sites to increase the housing supply and thereby reduce the backlog of minority
   candidates for housing who are displaced by slum
   clearance projects.

2. Raise income limits beyond the present maximum so
   as to receive a variety of income groups, races,
   colors, nationalities, etc.

3. Modify its policies of continuing occupancy as far
   as the statute and regulations may allow so as to
   permit tenants with higher incomes to remain in
   the projects.

4. Intensify its educational activities to attract the
   widest possible market among low-income families.

Public policy in line with these alternatives would
help prevent segregation without requiring the Authority
to determine the color of any individual. If the issue
could be resolved by such general policies, no further
discussion would be needed. But income limits are fixed
by federal policy and the selection of open sites meets the
resistance of white occupants and officialdom. Suppose,
despite all these plans and precautions, a project nevertheless heads toward occupancy by a particular minority.
May not the public agency then limit the number of Ne-

groes or Puerto Ricans or whites in order to effect an integrated pattern?

The question is a difficult one but the cases on discrimination should provide some guide. Good faith in the administration of laws is a relevant consideration and the courts have accepted the task of appraisal (*Brown* v. *the Board of Education of Topeka*, 349 US 294). The courts have also examined into the motives of public agencies in order to identify discriminatory practices. Thus in *Yick Wo* v. *Hopkins* (118 US 356), a San Francisco ordinance in the 1880s attempted to forbid the operation of laundries except in buildings of brick and stone, unless the City consented otherwise. Since the Chinese worked and lived in frame buildings, they would have been forced out of business. Though on the surface it all seemed a reasonable exercise of the police power, the Supreme Court looked behind the apparently innocent wording of the statute to discover its real intent in practice and declared it unconstitutional.

Motive in administration, therefore, cannot be dismissed lightly as part of the guiding criteria in the effort to find a way out of a legal dilemma. Motive is relevant in zoning and in the numerous other legal devices used to exclude or include minorities. What are called "quota systems" will inevitably be used by racists to exclude Negroes from white areas by a token admission to schools and housing, and will also be employed by well-intentioned officials and private builders to keep schools and neighborhoods from becoming segregated. If the underlying motive of a public agency is to prevent segregation in good faith, whether in schools or in housing, the means cannot be airily dismissed as irrelevant. Ends and means are part of a single package. When the Supreme Court, in ordering school desegregation in the South, ruled that it must be done with "deliberate speed," it was in fact ordering the local school boards to find the means by which to achieve the desired ends—even if the means implied looking at color. Nor, in measuring the "speed" with which integration is achieved in a segregated school, can the official be color-blind when he must identify the pupils whom he seeks to desegregate. When the ends of a device are to give token representation to the minority, the means and ends should be viewed as odious. It is otherwise when the means are employed to attain equality. Zoning, restrictive covenants, and slum clearance are not illegal *per se*, but they become illegal when the motive is corrupt. The confusion over the quota system is due primarily to the fact that the term is used at all, whether in its benign or its unbenign sense. It should be laid to rest.

The real reason that well-meaning officials have been forced into using devices such as "balancing communities" and "phase programs" is that discrimination exists in the policies of Federal and local governments. It is subtle but effective. It operates by omission and by failure to enact programs which can open housing to Negroes where they choose to live. The Negro is only 11.6 percent of the nation's population and about 50 percent of American Negroes are still in the South. If Congress, for example, enacted a law which made loans at nominal interest rates for home ownership as well as for public housing, there would be more chance of minorities enjoying the freedom to move, the denial of which enforces segregation. If the President's executive order in housing, now affecting less than a fifth of the nation's housing, were to be expanded to embrace savings and loan associations, more opportunity for ownership of private housing by Negroes would be possible. If income limits in public housing were increased, more white families would be eligible for what are now predominantly Negro-occupied projects. If suburbs were refused Federal loans for highways and housing as long as they persisted in exclusionary practices, there would be a better chance of their giving up their Mason-Dixon lines. If rental subsidies were afforded to less privileged families so that they could afford to compete for housing in suburbs as well as in central cities, segregation patterns in the central cities would diminish. If urban renewal and public works projects leveled fewer Negro areas, and if projects available to low-income families at subsidized rents could be built on open land there would be less tendency toward concentration by Negroes in the residual ghettos.

Since the New Deal days and its assumption of the general welfare power, the Federal Government has assumed the function of creating and implementing environment. It can influence that environment so that it is segregated or nonsegregated. It need not prescribe a preference for Negroes if the means are provided for all low-income families to gain access to decent housing in areas of their choice. The Negro would then automatically qualify, as would other underprivileged families. The Federal agencies should simultaneously see to it that the benefits of their loans and subsidies are not accorded to one race to the exclusion of another.

In short, the desegregation of communities is involved primarily with government policy and with the failure of that policy to effect a voluntary and what might lead to an automatic desegregation of neighborhoods. The so-called quota system is a symptom of the deficiencies of these national and state programs. Until these overlying deficiencies are corrected, public agencies and private builders attempting to grapple honestly with what is an almost impossible task merit a better understanding of their problems instead of a blanket condemnation.

EQUALITY

I

LOREN MILLER

Hurry, hurry sundown,

Let tomorrow come

... NEGRO BLUES SONG

One of the jests of American history texts is that crusty
old Thaddeus Stevens proposed to compensate former
slaves for what Abraham Lincoln called "two hundred
and fifty years of unrequited toil" by giving the head of
each family forty acres of land, to be carved out of the
holdings of dispossessed slaveholders. This first proposal
to give Negroes something of an even start with other
Americans went unheeded and the freedmen wound up
with the ballot and an imposing array of civil rights which
they lost in the South after Reconstruction had run its

Loren Miller is a Judge of the Municipal Court of Los
Angeles. He is at work on a history of the Supreme Court and
the Negro.

course. In 1963, almost a century later, and in the midst of another civil rights crisis, the National Urban League "challenged the responsible leadership of our country to undertake a massive 'Marshall Plan' approach of intensified special effort to close the wide economic, social and educational gap which separates the large majority of Negro citizens from other Americans." Whitney Young, League secretary, explained that his organization's fear was that Negroes would "wind up with a mouthful of civil rights and empty bellies, living in hovels." Charles Silberman, writing in *Fortune* magazine in March 1962, speculated that the nation might have to exercise some "positive discrimination" in favor of the Negro in order to close the gap that alarms the Urban League.

That gap is wide indeed. Let a government document give its main outlines:

[D]espite recent gains, large gaps continue to exist between white and nonwhite workers. . . .

Nonwhites continue to be concentrated in less-skilled jobs and are subject to more unemployment than whites. The jobless rates of nonwhites are still at least one and one half times higher than for whites in every age–sex grouping, and for some age groupings are three times as high. Unemployment bears disproportionately on the nonwhite worker whatever his industry or occupation. Not only is he subject to more frequent spells of unemployment; once out of a job he has tended to remain jobless for a longer period of time.

After achieving relatively substantial gains in money income during the early postwar period, *nonwhite families have failed to keep pace with the rise in average income of white families since the mid 1950's*, despite the shift of nonwhite workers into higher paying jobs.

During the past two decades, nonwhites have narrowed the educational gap that had historically existed between themselves and white persons. . . . *Since the mid-1950's, however, differences in the level of educational attainment between whites and nonwhites have remained essentially unchanged.*

The unemployment rate for nonwhites, at 11 percent in 1962, stood at its highest level in the postwar period. . . . Their *unemployment rate was double the jobless rate of white workers. This relationship has persisted throughout the postwar period.* [Italics added.]

That is what the Department of Labor said in July 1963. There is little to add except to underscore the fact that the trends are ominous, and to say that 44 percent of all Negro families lived in substandard housing in 1960 as compared to 13 percent for white families, and to remark that in the same year 80 percent of all Negro children were attending segregated and unequal schools. These statistics lend some credence to Stevens' argument of a century ago that "homesteads for [Negroes] now are more valuable than the immediate right of suffrage, although both are due" and that to "turn them loose unaided and unprotected" would be a "travesty on freedom and justice."

In fact, there was limited awareness of the need for special assistance to former slaves and some aid was extended through the Freedmen's Bureau. During the seven years of its existence, from 1865 to 1872, the Bureau spent more than five million dollars in establishing schools for freedmen, which enrolled 150,000 pupils and employed some 3300 teachers. This Bureau also dispensed direct aid to the tune of more than eight million "rations" and undertook to guarantee fairness in contracts entered into between Negroes and employers. These activities excited some opposition, but the Bureau ran into heavy trouble through its policy of leasing forty-acre tracts of "abandoned" or confiscated land to Negro heads of families, one of the very purposes for which it had been established. Under the Act of 1865, the Bureau was authorized to lease to every male Negro, "whether refugee or freedman," not more than forty acres of "land within the insurrectionary states as shall have been abandoned, or to which the United States shall have acquired title by confiscation or sale" for a three-year period at an annual rental of 6 percent of its appraised value as of 1860, and to sell the land to the lessee at its 1860 value at the end of the lease. As former slaveholders were pardoned or received amnesty, they reclaimed the "abandoned" land and confiscations were set aside. Negro lessees were promptly evicted or reduced to being renters of former owners and their purchase rights terminated.

The precariously based and limited land reform program collapsed. Intransigent Southern opposition met no matching fervor from Abolitionists-turned-Republicans who regarded their duty as done with the grant of freedom and civil rights to Negroes. The concept of special treatment for a disadvantaged group was foreign to American political thought. The Constitution postulated a society of equals in which every individual by the exercise of thrift, perseverance, and hard work was capable of making his own way. The Republican program extended that individual equality to Negroes through the guarantees of citizenship, due process, and equal protection of the law embodied in the Fourteenth Amendment, and by the right of suffrage bestowed in the Fifteenth Amendment, complemented by supporting congressional legislation. Therefore, ran the argument, the Negro would be able to, and should, shift for himself like any other American. In time he would overcome his transitional handicaps. Of course, he would need education but he could secure it on a plane of equality with all others as he exercised his right of franchise and participated in the political affairs of his state and community. Moreover—and in some sense, above all—the equalitarian guarantees of the Constitution accrued to individuals, to *persons* in constitutional language, and not to groups. The Civil War Amendments, which removed inequalities theretofore visited on Negroes, *as Negroes*, did not and could not bestow benefits on Negroes *as Negroes*. The Constitution was color-blind. So was opportunity.

We have not yet moved beyond that concept. We are still saying that the Negro needs education and that he can get an education on a parity with all other Americans if we safeguard his civil rights and remove voting barriers so that he can participate fully in the affairs of the nation, the state, and the community. The Negro can, we assure ourselves again, overcome transitional handicaps by thrift, hard work, and perseverance. We still conceive of equalitarian guarantees of the Constitution as accruing to individuals, to *persons*, and not to groups and we cling to the belief that the Constitution which forbids imposition of inequality because of group membership likewise forbids special assistance to members of a group. We must, we say with increasing emphasis and frequency, make the Constitution color-blind, and under the beneficence of a color-blind Constitution, we shall conjure up color-blind opportunity for all Americans. The suggestion that the nation undertake special measures to assist Negroes is rebuffed as "discrimination in reverse."

There are no *ifs* in history and we cannot know with certainty what would have happened had the Civil War Amendments been given the full scope intended by their framers, with Negroes exercising to the very limit their full civil rights and the privilege of voting freely and without restrictions. What we do know is that the America into which the freedmen emerged was an America of expanding individual opportunity, increasingly in need of industrial labor and feverishly beckoning to European immigrants to come to its shores and help build a nation; that it was just beginning to tap its vast natural resources which would enrich thousands and offer economic well-being to millions of others. We know that many of the immigrants who poured into this country overcame initial handicaps of ignorance, illiteracy, and even prejudice against them, and that their progeny are now represented in all strata of American life from the very rich to the very poor.

The Abolitionist dream, sustained by a belief in the

Rights of Man, was that after the end of slavery, with the
grant of citizenship rights and the ballot, racial identification would become as unimportant as eye color or height
of the individual—as is true in Latin America. If we discard belief in racial inferiority, we can surmise that reali-
zation of this dream was not an impossibility and that we
would not now be plagued with the problem of a racial
gap. No such thing happened. Instead, a color-caste
system developed out of the ruins of slavery, isolating
descendants of slaves and excluding them from the mainstream of American life almost to the same extent that
their forefathers had been isolated and excluded as slaves.
A century after Emancipation, we are still fumbling with
the problem of how to implement the promise of racial
equality we thought we had realized with the passage of
the Civil War Amendments. Whitney Young's estimate
of the manner in which we can achieve that end in today's
urban society coincides in principle with Thaddeus Stevens' proposal for its solution in the Southern agricultural
order of a hundred years ago. Obviously, we need to examine and understand the reasons for our century of in-
eptitude.

Stevens was rewarded for his foresight by the hoots
and jeers of most of his contemporaries; opponents
sneered at him for offering Negroes "forty acres and a
mule" in order to further the fortunes of the Republican
party. Historians still point to his proposed reform as *the*
horrible example of an attempt to punish the South for
having lost a glamorous war to preserve States' rights. A

decade after Stevens' death, Benjamin "Pap" Singleton, styling himself its Moses, founded what he called the Exodus, a movement to lead landless and hopeless Negroes out of the South and to the frontier where the Federal Government was giving away quarter sections of land to homesteaders. Southern landowners interested in cheap labor registered violent objections, the Federal Government wasn't concerned, Negroes were too disorganized to respond, and the movement fizzled out after some 40,000 former slaves had straggled westward. The majority of rural freedmen settled down in the South to sharecropping and service as farm laborers, where the Jim Crow system ultimately froze them in a social and economic status a notch or two lower than their poverty-stricken white counterparts.

Negroes began voting with their feet against the new plantation system by migrating in substantial numbers to Southern and border cities in the late 1880s and 1890s, only to find discrimination that differed in degree and not in kind from what they had known down on the farm. When they picked up and moved further North after the turn of the century, they found white workingmen hostile. The new American Federation of Labor under the leadership of another immigrant, Samuel Gompers, shut them out. Industry found the colored migrants handy for occasional strike-breaking chores but preferred the apparently endless supply of European immigrants as steady employees. Industrialists balanced the scales after a fashion by making gifts to Booker T. Washington's Tuskegee Institute and other vocational schools where Negroes were taught handicraft skills to fit them for the age of mass production. In the long run, urban Negro workmen, North and South, were shunted off into unskilled and unorganized menial jobs or found employment for themselves, or their wives, as domestics. They did establish a few beachheads in better-paying skilled positions during World War I, but the depression of the 1930s wiped out most of those gains.

Meanwhile, the United States Supreme Court had chipped in with the 1896 "separate but equal" decision in *Plessy* v. *Ferguson*, holding in essence that Chief Justice Roger Taney was correct when he noted in the famed Dred Scott cases that under the Constitution, "The unhappy black race were separated from the white by indelible marks." The 1896 Court said that the law was "powerless to eradicate racial instincts or to abolish distinctions based on physical differences" and held that the states—and the Federal Government, for that matter— were constitutionally justified in classifying citizens on the basis of race and forbidding their use of state facilities, private accommodations, and public utilities on the basis of that classification. It added that where Negroes were excluded from state facilities or private utilities, they must be furnished separate and equal accommodations for their own use, a hedge that was construed to mean that a one-room Negro school in a church basement was equal to a graded eight-room school for whites and that Jim Crow seats in half of a baggage car were equal to Pullman accommodations. The governmental example stiffened the backbones of private groups: labor unions, churches, YMCAs, PTAs, Rotary Clubs, trade associations, professional organizations, the Knights of Columbus, Masons, Elks, Shriners, and college fraternities, to pick a few random examples, tightened up their rituals and by-laws and drew ever more rigid color lines. The Navy banished Negroes to the steward's branch of the service, the Marine Corps excluded them, and the Army segregated them. Organized baseball, the most American of all sports, became lily white.

Negroes kept on trooping into the cities. As the unwanted and strangers always do, these new city dwellers huddled together and soon, North and South, found themselves hemmed up in ghettos which spawned segregated schools and other public and semipublic facilities. Government—local, state and Federal—heightened the ghetto walls by judicial enforcement of racial restrictive covenants, manipulation of zoning rules and ordinances, and after 1934 by the segregatory devices of Federal housing agencies, and bred an almost insatiable demand for more and more residential segregation. "Would-you-want-one-to-live-next-door-to-you?" became the Northern and Western equivalent of the Southern "Would-you-want-your-sister-to-marry-one?" The answer was a resounding no. Banks and lending institutions tailored their policies to the maintenance of the Black Belt. The National Association of Real Estate Boards made social pariahs of brokers who violated the taboo by selling to a Negro outside the ghetto. Landlords and owners neglected upkeep on their Black Belt property, always readily salable in a protected seller's market. Overuse and overcrowding hastened its deterioration. Municipal authorities, hard put to raise adequate tax money for street repair, school construction, and other public purposes, could seldom resist the pressure of middle-class white communities for the lion's share of public funds. The ghetto became a slum at worst, or at best a decaying, neglected neighborhood.

Hope died unborn for unnumbered thousands of Negro youngsters as the ghetto gave back to them images of themselves as the inferiors they were supposed to be by the vast majority of other Americans. In their anger and frustration, bewildered and case-hardened Negroes, young and old, strengthened the charges preferred against them by violating the canons of middle-class morality by which they were judged, thus "establishing" the popular case that such people were not fit to live in neighborhoods with good schools and excellent environment. Confined in the Northern and Western urban ghettos, Negroes at least had the vote and could send out ambassadors in the shape of elected representatives to barter for their rights in city councils or state legislatures. In the South, the Negro was not only denied the right to vote but had to suffer the indignity of serving as a whipping boy for politicians who sought public office; the candidate who promised to degrade him most became his governor, or mayor, or senator —his representative!

The rigid color-caste system created a thin middle class

of lawyers, doctors, businessmen, teachers, preachers, and the like to minister to the needs of the rank and file. These, who liked to think of themselves as the "Talented Tenth" (a term chosen by W. E. B. Du Bois), formed organizations such as the NAACP and the Urban League to safeguard and widen the small freedoms Negroes enjoyed. In the North, the emergent middle class began winning elective offices from Negro constituencies in the 1920s and wangled political appointments for a few of its members; it participated in the uneasy alliance of the 1930s and 1940s that elected Franklin D. Roosevelt and Harry S. Truman to the Presidency and, in turn, shared in appointments to the agencies that sprang up in the new welfare state. It traded and dickered with its new labor allies to pry open union doors to Negro workmen, too often on a token basis. NAACP lawyers shrewdly capitalized on the burgeoning Supreme Court liberalism of the New Deal and Fair Deal and pressed the case for new constitutional interpretations that would revitalize the Civil War Amendments. The times were propitious for change: there was a ferment of reform in the world and in the land and, equally important, scholars had riddled the outworn dogmas of racial inferiority and superiority. As World War II approached, Hitler's excesses held up a mirror to the nation and many saw clearly that American racism was as indefensible as Nazi anti-Semitism.

As World War II swept thousands of them into the armed forces Negroes opened a "Double V" program: victory over Hitler abroad, victory over racial discrimination at home. Roosevelt was pressured into establishing the nation's first fair employment code. Industry, in dire need of workmen, dipped into the Negro labor pool and siphoned off almost everybody who was willing to work. The Army, the Navy, the new Air Force, and even the Marine Corps dropped color barriers. All over the world, Negro servicemen sampled small doses of freedom and found the taste heady and good. Cities, great and small, in crucial states bulged with Negro migrants who could vote and politicians came bearing gifts—or at least promises—of civil rights. At war's end, race relations were in a state of flux. As the Jim Crow curtain parted, Negroes caught a new vision of the promised land of first-class citizenship.

In a series of decisions during and after World War II, the Supreme Court, responding to the pleas of a devoted group of brilliant NAACP lawyers, invalidated the white primary, forbade racial segregation by interstate carriers, interdicted judicial enforcement of racial housing covenants, re-enforced rules against exclusion of Negroes from juries, and prohibited exclusion from and segregation of Negroes in graduate and professional schools, thus undermining the "separate but equal" rule. States and cities began strengthening public accommodation statutes and enacting first fair employment and then fair housing laws and ordinances. Segregation was abolished as the rule in the armed forces. Racial barriers fell in professional sports and in a wide range of voluntary organizations. In every assault on exclusionary and discriminatory practices, the Negro middle class, led by the NAACP, had the active aid and assistance of organized labor, political liberals, and religious groups. In 1954 the Supreme Court swept the "separate but equal" rule into the discard with its decision ordering the end of segregation in public schools and by subsequent rulings invalidating segregatory laws affecting parks, playgrounds, libraries, golf courses, and other public facilities. In 1957 Congress enacted the first civil rights bill since Reconstruction. The NAACP celebrated its apparent triumph by adopting a new slogan: "Free in '63." The celebration was premature.

War's end brought other changes. As employment declined and white veterans returned, Negro workmen, as the last hired, lost jobs by the working of the seniority system and subtle prejudices. Automation was speeded up and began taking its racial toll. By 1958 the rate of Negro unemployment had doubled that of whites and reached the depression level of approximately 10 percent, where it has remained. New all-white suburbs, some of them cities in themselves, girdled cities and towns and trapped Negroes in rapidly expanding central city ghettos. By 1960 more than four million of the nation's nineteen million Negroes lived in segregated communities in its ten largest cities; more Negro children attended all-Negro schools in those cities than in Mississippi, Alabama, and South Carolina combined. Urban relief rolls were clogged with Negro recipients. Negro crime and juvenile delinquency figures climbed, absolutely out of proportion to whites'. Taking advantage of the Supreme Court's "deliberate speed" formula, Southern states almost nullified the order for school desegregation, and found new devices to bolster the Jim Crow system in transportation and in the use of public accommodations and state facilities. The bright dream of equality was tarnished anew.

In 1955 a tired Negro woman unaccountably refused to move to the rear of a Montgomery, Alabama, bus and suddenly a boycott movement erupted, with Negroes walking for freedom in the footsteps of Martin Luther King, who preached a strange new message of nonviolence. The echoes of that march had not died before two Negro students sat down in a white hamburger stand in North Carolina in 1960. A rash of sit-ins, wade-ins, pray-ins, and lie-ins broke out, forcing an astounding number of Southern places of public accommodation and even churches to wipe out exclusionary practices. Other students, flouting laws, ordinances, and custom, embarked on Freedom Rides in the heart of the Deep South. Outside the South, the nation nodded approval.

Emboldened Negroes took to the streets to demonstrate —to offer their bodies as living witness to their desire for Freedom Now, they said. And a crisis overtook the nation. It came to climax in Birmingham in 1963 and whether the point of no return was the dogs straining at their leashes for a taste of human flesh, or Bull Connor shouting to reporters to "come and see the niggers run," or the fire hoses flushing men, women, and children off the streets, or the completely symbolic picture of a white cop with his knee on a Negro woman's throat, we will never know. Whatever it was, Birmingham put the segregation system to its ultimate test and observant Americans, white and black alike, knew that the old order was threshing around on its deathbed. Again the North began nodding approval, but the chorus of approbation died in its throat as demonstrations flared in New York, Chicago, Philadelphia, Los Angeles, and a half dozen other cities whose residents *knew* that *their* Negroes were happy and content with the progress that was being made in race relations. These demonstrations welled up from below and caught the Negro middle class and its liberal allies off guard; the rules of the game had been changed without their consent, almost without their knowledge. The Negro revolution had begun.

All revolutions have slogans and the slogan of the Negro revolution was "Freedom Now," but the words did not encompass the entire change in Negro thinking and attitude. A new content had been added to the century-old cry for civil rights; the term had been altered and expanded to include, in addition to the privileges of using public accommodations and casting a ballot, a demand for elimination of all discriminatory patterns in American social, economic, and educational life. Northern demonstrators were revolting against unemployment; the strait jacket of relief rolls; the institutionalized discrimination of the employer, the labor union, and civil service; the ghetto, with its compulsory segregation in schools and other public facilities; and, above all, against the arrangement of American life that disadvantaged the Negro from the cradle to the grave. And Freedom Now meant that he no longer wanted "progress" in race relations; he wanted an even start with all other Americans—now, today, under his own leadership and direction and on his own terms. A long day's journey lay ahead.

In June 1963, one hundred years and six months after the Emancipation Proclamation, President John F. Kennedy surveyed the scene and pronounced the melancholy factual judgment that:

The Negro baby born in America today, regardless of the section in which he is born, has about one half as much chance of completing high school as a white baby, one third as much chance of completing college, one third as much chance of becoming a professional man, twice as much chance of becoming unemployed, one seventh as much chance of earning $10,000 a year, a life expectancy which is seven years shorter, and the prospects of earning only half as much.

The President's words were not the dispassionate pronouncements of a Chief Executive made after quiet study of a social problem. They were wrenched from him after Birmingham in an effort to still what he called the "rising tide of discontent that threatens the public safety" and to warn Americans that "It is a time to act in the Congress, in State and local legislative bodies and, above all, in all of our daily lives."

The first and most obvious need was for congressional legislation to implement the equalitarian purposes of the Fourteenth Amendment. In June 1963 President Kennedy proposed a package deal to Congress. Congress acted. For the first time in history, the Senate choked off a civil rights filibuster in June 1964, and passed the Civil

Rights Act a year after the presidential message. We have taken a long stride with the civil rights legislation of 1964, but there are chinks in that legislative armor. Even if it were perfect, we are met with the fact, noted by Eli Ginzburg, that "If the color barriers could be eliminated overnight, that fact alone would not materially improve the position of the Negro." More is needed. That more in terms of immediate need is the elimination of the "gap which separates the large majority of Negro citizens from other Americans." It cannot be achieved merely by the passage of equalitarian legislation that would wipe out all distinctions between Negroes and white Americans and place them on an even footing from now on. The back wheels never catch up with the front wheels on the same buggy, as the expressive Negro idiom has it. Phrasing the problem doesn't solve it.

Whitney Young offers no specifics in his plea for a "massive Marshall Plan" but the implication is that he favors Silberman's *Fortune* magazine suggestion that "The U.S. must come to look upon the Negro community as if it were an underdeveloped country." Paule Murray, author and lawyer, expressed the same idea to Radcliffe alumnae: "If the United States can spend billions of dollars in foreign aid to help bring less developed countries abreast of the modern age, it can at least offer comparable assistance to a deprived sector of its own citizenry. We need 'Operation Bootstrap' which engages in massive national effort to raise the hopes and standards of the forgotten part of our population. . . ."

If the nation's nineteen million Negroes and all their property were tucked neatly away in a country of their own on the coast of Africa or some island in the sea, their commonwealth would rate a high priority in our foreign aid program. Theirs would be a country with a better than 90 percent basic literacy rate; with a preponderance of unskilled and agricultural workers, a fair number of skilled workers, and a goodly proportion of lawyers, doctors, schoolteachers, and civil servants, all of them English speaking and practically all of them with a deep commitment to the democratic way of life. One of the high priorities might be given to wiping out educational deficiencies.

There is no reason why such a program could not be initiated in the American educational system to aid Negroes. Initial experiments with compensatory education have been fruitful in Harlem and other Negro centers. A crash program in this area would certainly be expensive, but hardly as costly as the present large crop of dropouts and inadequately trained Negro pupils scrounging around on urban streets. Northern and Western states may be induced to embark on such programs, but only Federal aid and stimulation can be looked to in Southern states. We might hope that in a decade Negro youngsters would have training equal to that of their white counterparts. There is no suggestion here that every Negro youngster will turn out to be a superior product, but the overwhelming odds are that compensatory education would produce a substantial number of students whose social contributions would far exceed the cost of their education and training.

An even higher priority must be given to the problem of employment, even if the first objective is the limited one of raising the level of Negro employment to that of white Americans—that is, eliminating the gap between the unemployment rate of whites and Negroes. At the threshold, we are met with the bland assumption that all of the Negro's employment ills can be traced to the fact that he is less prepared than others. This is an ingenious partial truth resting on another assumption that there is an absolute standard by which applicants for employment can be measured and the most competent chosen. That may be true in the most highly skilled trades, but there is no such standard for most white-collar and blue-collar employees; the entrant meets a minimum standard and attains skill and competence by experience. The truth is that the most important, albeit unarticulated, major standard for initial employability is race, as it has been for the past century. The image of the desirable and desired worker is that of the white employee whose smiling face beams at us from advertisements on TV, on billboards, in the movies, and wherever else *the* American workman is portrayed. He or she gets the first call at the factory gate or in the hiring hall, and the endless repetition of this small preference has snowballed into an imposing imbalance of white employment. This process is halted, even reversed, where the Negro gets a fairly even chance in civil service, as in urban postal service, where there is a disproportion of Negro employees, even in the South. Negroes are some

11 percent of the total work force but comprise about 15.3 percent of those in the postal service.

Where testing is used in civil service, it is agreed that there is no practical difference insofar as expected performance goes between the man who scores 95.2 to place first and the man who rates 85.2 for third place. The appointing authority may choose one of the first three, even if the third man got his rating by a gratuitous grant of ten points for veteran status. In that situation, we are agreeing that there is no practical difference as to performance expectation between the man who rates 75.2 on a test and the man who earned a 95.2 score. We agree with this estimate in civil service procedures, even where there is no issue of racial preference. However, if the employee choice were being made by a private employer, who is not bound by results of tests and who may give none, the pretext for his choice would be that the white applicant who rated 95.2 by some subjective analysis was absolutely entitled to the job over the Negro who rated a lower score. The person who suggested that a Negro third on the list by the employer's subjective judgment should be hired, in order to correct racial imbalance resulting from prior discrimination, would be set upon by unions and even well-meaning liberals and accused of demanding "discrimination in reverse."

One of the differences between the employment figures in private industry and in a civil service apparatus such as the postal service arises from the fact that the private employer often selects employees from an almost totally white labor pool. A number of interconnected factors are at play: (1) the persistence of the image of the white workman as the desirable employee; (2) the failure of industry to seek out and recruit Negro workmen; (3) the timidity, or worse, of the discouraged Negro workman to present himself as a competitor for available employment; and (4) the demand, often subconscious, that the Negro who is considered for employment must be better than his white prototype—the tacit assumption of racial superiority that demands that every Negro civil servant be a Ralph Bunche and every Negro ballplayer a Jackie Robinson. A compensatory employment policy—what Charles Silberman calls "positive discrimination in favor of the Negro"—is the first requisite in wiping out the employment gap. Industry must obliterate the image of the white workman as *the* desirable employee, recruit Negro employees with the same intensity and ingenuity it used in World War II, and drop the demand for superiority as a condition for Negro employment. The Negro workman must be prodded into an aggressive quest for employment despite past refusals.

Employers must go beyond these guideposts and adopt what civil service regards as a truism: that in the area of ordinary skills, hiring need not be offered on the basis of the highest score of the applicants. Despite purist fears, such a program does not require individual discrimination; what it does comprehend is the pulling and pushing forward of Negroes as a group into the labor market and thus placing the individual Negro in a position where he can be and *is* hired. It calls for a reversal of racial roles: where whites as a group are now, and long have been, preferred, Negroes as a group get the preference. As Henry Steeger, Urban League president, phrases it: "The white population of this country has been in a preferential position for some 200 years. So it would not seem out of order to suggest at least ten years of special effort for Negro citizens." Steeger's sweet reasonableness will not deter opposition, grounded in custom or tradition, and seeming to threaten the advantage, real or fancied, now enjoyed by beneficiaries of the old order, whether employers or unions.

Union resistance to compensatory or preferential employment may be even more determined than that of employers. In New York City, for example, the AFL–CIO plumbers union went on strike when three Negro and one Puerto Rican plumbers were hired on a city installation. The complaint was that the nonwhites were not members of the union and that union rolls were not open at the time. The union ultimately had its way when the nonwhite plumbers were jockeyed into taking an examination and failed to pass the test. The results were hailed as proof that employment was afforded on a merit basis and the Negroes were told, in effect, to lift themselves by their own bootstraps to the standard of their white competitors. The unspoken premise was that every white union plumber could have taken the examination and passed with flying colors. That is doubtful, even after their years of experience gained at the expense of Negroes; but, even if so, there is no proof that the examination offers an absolute standard for employability for work to be done on the particular job. In fact, the ousted Negroes were doing satisfactory work on the job. It must be observed that the nonwhites were not competing in an open test against white plumbers and nobody knows how they would have ranked in such an open examination, or what the results would have been had the civil service rule-of-three been applied. An examination of the kind given was an exclusionary device, not an attempt to draw Negro plumbers into the work force; it was an obvious, and successful, attempt to insulate time-honored union discrimination from attack.

It is unreasonable to suppose that employers are going to abandon old policies easily, especially where union opposition crops up. Governmental leadership must be exerted. Such leadership can be exerted effectively where the employer is engaged on government contracts. Under the plans-for-progress program of the President's Committee on Equal Employment Opportunity, government has recognized that the employer must do more than post a sign proclaiming that he is an "equal opportunity employer." The progress program requires periodic checkups, with reports on the results obtained in employment of nonwhites, a tacit recognition that the employer must seek out and recruit Negro workmen. The process should not stop there; government itself should embark on an intensive program to encourage Negro application for jobs. And as the Negro labor pool is enlarged through recruitment and Negro application, government must encourage—"pressure" is probably a better word—employers to hire Negro applicants. In the highly skilled trades, apprentice programs must be pried open to admit Negro trainees, even at the expense of doing violence to present union subscription to hereditary rules which pass jobs down to sons, nephews, and relatives of men who got their positions as a result of racial discrimination. Here again, the key is governmental pressure, recruitment, and encouragement, and frank acknowledgment of the envisaged end.

If government is to lead and pressure for this policy, it must have clean hands in its own employment practices. An inspection of civil service will show that it bears sins of its own. The problem in civil service is that Negroes are too often frozen in the lower reaches. As the Commission on Civil Rights has pointed out, there are "Negro" jobs and "white" jobs in the Federal service, and the same thing holds true for municipal and state services. In the postal service, for example, where Negroes constitute about 15 percent of the field service, only a handful are in supervisory positions, despite supposedly fair promotion policies and relative imbalance of better educated Negroes. An overhaul of promotional practices is imperative, with an open, announced policy of preference for Negroes who do qualify for promotion or who can be reached under the rule of selection of one of the first three on the list. Only rigid and ruthless pursuit of such a policy can undo decades of a similar, but concealed, policy of favoritism for whites. Promotional tests need revision; they are too often—almost universally—deliberately designed to establish a white hierarchy. So long as that hierarchy has its way, it will order its own white succession.

There are other areas of governmental employment in which admission depends on recruitment policy and where racial complexion can be changed by a change in recruiting procedures, as the Kennedy administration proved. The Kennedys were able to find able Negro administrators and lesser employees simply because they looked for them. On the political level, for example, they found two Negro district attorneys, where the previous rule had been that Negro lawyers served only in minor deputy positions. They found two Negro district judges where none had served before. The State Department had been a lily-white preserve until Kennedy policies demanded safaris to Negro colleges and other likely sources. The list could be extended, but the surface has been barely scratched on a Federal level and has been disturbed even less on state and local levels. Wherever change has been induced, it has been triggered by racial surveys to find out just how many Negroes are on the payroll, over the anguished cries of administrators that they don't keep racial records and know nothing of the race of employees. In almost every instance, surveys have shown that these know-nothing administrators have been presiding over predominantly white departments. A change in recruitment policies worked wonders in most instances. Preferential employment in favor of Negroes speeded the change. More needs to be done along the same line.

Obviously, governmental policy of the kind outlined above is bound to raise bitter opposition, with the claim that government ought not to single out a group for special favors. The claim is not as invulnerable as it seems to be. Large-scale hire-the-handicapped programs are undertaken without objection; yet loss of a leg is often less of a handicap than being born with a dark skin, and physical handicaps have not been deliberately inflicted as have racial handicaps. Government has been enthusiastic about pressing the case for veteran preference in employment, even to the extent of granting extra points in civil service tests, because we realize that the veteran has been penalized by having to devote time to military service. There, too, the nation compensates for the imposition of a social handicap. We boggle at applying the same rules to Negroes only because we disregard or misread history and refuse to admit that the nation has imposed disabling burdens on Negroes for irrational reasons.

In another area of employment, CORE director James Farmer has urged a large-scale public works program calculated to employ Negroes, a proposal concurred in by Paule Murray. Here, again, specifics are lacking but the idea seems to have been somewhat anticipatory of President Johnson's antipoverty program. However, Farmer's proposal was directed toward undertaking a cleaning up and refurbishing of the nation's urban Black Belts out of the belief that any such make-work program would also result in betterment of housing and public facilities where the need is great and where success would have the double social impact of furnishing jobs and lifting the level of urban living. In the ordinary case, a public works program would not single out Negroes for employment. However, if jobs were made available to the unemployed or under-employed, Negroes would benefit out of proportion to other groups of the population simply because they are overrepresented on the unemployment rolls. Any program that strikes at poverty is bound to offer maximum aid to the most poverty-stricken. Negroes fall in that category. Here, preference is the inevitable result of the workings of past policies: Jim Crow flaps home to roost.

A program which did offer compensatory employment to Negroes would have to surmount constitutional and legal hurdles and would meet the objection that the equal protection clause of the Fourteenth Amendment restrains the grant of benefits to members of one group that are not extended to all persons alike. In some respects, the objection is more apparent than real. There is a substantial body of employment law, developed in labor cases, to the effect (1) that there is an obligation to overcome present effects of past discrimination, (2) that this obligation exists even if discrimination was not illegal at the time of inception, and (3) that the effects may be overcome despite hardships to innocent parties. In those industries and unions where there is a provable and historic pattern of racial discrimination, these principles would seem to apply and should become the code for change and correction. Enforcement might run counter to seniority rules and to "grandfather" policies of unions that have dropped "white only" clauses in their constitutions and rituals but continue discrimination by limiting membership to relatives of old members or to recruits recommended by members. The courts have held that employees have no vested right in seniority rules. Those rules whose enforcement imposes discrimination can be abrogated by law without offending constitutional requirements. And unions are not social clubs; their "grandfather" policies can be forbidden with impunity, just as similar voting prescriptions were invalidated by the courts. Union control of apprentice admissions has been expedited through recommendations of participants based on relationships or discriminatory whim. Corrective statutory action would be appropriate; indeed, a Federal court in Chicago recently ordered three Negro apprentices admitted to a program in which it was found that the union had made discriminatory selections. Most of these objectives can be pursued within the framework of existing state fair employment laws, if fair employment is seen as requiring more than correction of individual injustices.

These limited correctives do not meet the issue of whether benign racial classification undertaken to correct discriminatory practices can escape the stricture of the equal protection clause. At the outset, it is well to recognize that the Fourteenth Amendment was corrective: it was a command to the states not only to drop discriminatory laws and customs supported by law, but to take affirmative action to confer equality on Negroes. The original intent was that where the states failed to act, that obligation would devolve on the Federal Government. When Congress tried to act in the context of its own times through the passage of civil rights laws and other equalitarian statutes, the Supreme Court misread the Amendment to limit the requirement of equal protection to those situations in which the states imposed inequality. A return to the Fourteenth Amendment requires a reinstatement of the original purpose. The multiplication of inequality through a century of governmental tolerance and support of the color-caste system can be ameliorated only through frank recognition that the result of treating the Negro differently has made the Negro's status in American life different from that of other Americans. Negroes must be assisted *as Negroes*, just as they have been disadvantaged *as Negroes*, if the Amendment is to serve its equalitarian purpose. After all, we treat women *as women* in minimum wage and hour laws for their protection; children *as children* in child labor laws; and veterans *as veterans* in veteran preference legislation. We were deterred from protecting women and children for decades by the specious argument that to do so would invade the law of contracts which, it was argued, must have universal and equal application to all laborers. Only when we discarded these fanciful "fair on their face" notions in favor of benign classifications based on social realities were we able to cope with the evils of the sweatshop and child labor. Ultimately, we must face the social realities of racial classification in order to overcome its evils.

Meanwhile, a way out of the constitutional impasse may be found through use of the principle embodied in Federal legislation designed to assist depressed areas and President Johnson's proposal to lift Appalachia out of the mire of poverty and dependence. Sprawling Negro ghettos in every large and small city, with their chronic unemployment, their overt representation on relief rolls, their crime and delinquency problems, their need for education, and their lack of ready avenues for employment *are* depressed areas, yet they do not qualify under existing legislation because they are lumped with advantaged sections of their city to take the larger community out of the depressed-area classification. Legislation which extended the depressed-area label to include geographical sections of metropolitan complexes could bring Negro communities within a permissible classification, because race would not ostensibly be the basis. Since 72 percent of the nation's Negroes live in urban areas, almost three-quarters of the Negro population could be reached in that manner. Rural poverty and deprivation are largely concentrated in the South's Black Belt counties, and an extension of the depressed-area concept to include particular rural areas would include them.

Compensatory assistance for urban Black Belts could be provided by resort to a crash public works program designed to offer employment and to refurbish these ghettos. Renovation of these blighted sections will not only better housing conditions of present Negro inhabitants and afford them new and better schools and public recreational and other facilities, but would also serve to attract whites back into the central city—and thus to undermine residential segregation. We are only dabbling at urban renewal and redevelopment at the moment; we could put the idea to full and complete social use under such a program, provided we were willing to open up the housing market and use suburban undeveloped land to construct housing for those displaced in the process of rebuilding. Here, again, we would strike a blow at the ghetto. Of course, economically depressed urban areas of all kinds would have to be encompassed in enabling legislation, but we should face up to the fact that what we are after is compensatory assistance to Negroes now trapped in the ghetto and that we are heeding Silberman's advice "to look upon the Negro community as if it were an underdeveloped country." In effect, that is what President Johnson proposes in the case of Appalachia—the underdeveloped country has even been given a name. Assistance is thus lifted out of the category of charity and presented for what it is: an effort to put residents of the area back on their feet so that they can become self-sustaining. In short, the President proposes to close the gap between Appalachians and other Americans and there is no pretense that the job can be done by simply treating them on a plane of equality with others. He projects preferential treatment for them. Appalachia stands in no greater need of preferential treatment than our urban Black Belts, and we must adopt the same attitude toward them. Such an attitude would put the problem in proper perspective and

give social motivation to what might otherwise be regarded as a gigantic boondoggle.

We aid underdeveloped nations as a matter of national
policy, partly because we think it is to our best interest to
accelerate their growth and development as responsible
members of the world community, partly because of our
moral commitment to help our neighbors, and partly because we think it is good business. Those same considerations undergird suggestions for an internal "Marshall
Plan" to aid Negroes as a group in our internal social
order. The air is filled with complaints about the irresponsibility of Negroes as citizens; understandable de-
linquencies in that regard will multiply unless we eliminate
the ghetto traps that breed irresponsibility. The American
moral commitment to wipe out three centuries of racial
discrimination hardly needs emphasis. And there is every
evidence that raising the Negro's economic status would
be good business indeed.

Best estimates are that the current annual Negro market
for consumer goods is around 12 billion dollars. That
market is underdeveloped in comparison to the white
market because the median annual income for Negro
males is $3075, as compared to $5137 for the white male
worker; that for Negro women is $1276, in comparison
with $2537 for the white female worker. Using these
statistics as a base, the Urban League's Commerce and
Industry Council, headed by Winthrop Rockefeller, estimates that "if the nation's seven million non-white working forces were earning the same median income as the

white working force, the yearly personal income would be increased by $12 billion—or nearly double its present level." The Council computes the Gross National Product loss as a result of discrimination at 14 billion dollars, consisting of more than 11 billion dollar losses to individuals; a 350 million dollar loss to industry through losses on corporate profits, dividends, net interest, and wage accruals; and a product loss of more than 2 billion dollars. The Council maintains that the nation loses at least "$28 billion every year" because "for every dollar lost in 'new income' because of the race problem, the nation must also spend an existing dollar to compensate for the present ill effects of that problem." The estimated extra annual expense caused by discrimination is put at almost 2 billion dollars, through expenditure of 300 million dollars for aid to dependent children, 250 million dollars for public assistance to the aged, 500 million dollars for aid to the unemployed, and 500 million dollars for correctional programs.

Obviously, such increased earnings would be a boon to Negroes, but they would also redound to the advantage of all Americans. Walter H. Heller, chairman of the national Council of Economic Advisers, estimates that if the added wages were pumped into the national economy, the Gross National Product would be raised some 2.5 percent. At a time when foreign aid has not borne the expected fruit and when ever-increasing military expenditures become a greater and greater drag on the economy, the development of the internal Negro market would provide an important economic shot in the arm. The inevitable stimulation of consumer industries attendant on satisfaction of dammed-up Negro needs would ultimately be reflected in gains for the white workman. The estimate is that an added 12 billion dollar market, gained by raising the Negro wage level to that of whites, would put 1.5 billion dollars into the housing industry, another 1.2 billion dollars into automobile and transportation purchases, and 1.7 billion dollars into the clothing industry annually —to pick only a few examples. It would also be accompanied by a decrease in social services that now burden the taxpayer. Equality would pay off in prosperity.

The sum of the whole matter is that the nation has run up a big bill in developing and supporting racial inequality. We must pay some time, and the longer we delay, the greater the accrued interest. The alternative does not lie between escaping or discharging the debt, but between the means and time of payment; every demonstration reminds us anew that Birmingham voiced the death rattle of the old order. Judicial invalidation of the "separate but equal" rule, state equalitarian legislation, and the new Federal civil rights laws were prerequisites to effective action on social and economic problems. We could do little so long as we kept the Negro in a condition of inferior citizenship. We can depend on the NAACP to press the case against second-class citizenship with increasing vigor with the new weapons at its command. Political roads to change are now open.

In the final analysis, the Negro wants, and has demanded, his civil rights because he believes that their exercise will enable him to share in all that America has to offer, and has offered, white Americans. The Negro revolution, which began as a protest against segregation and denial of the franchise and other elementary civil rights, quickly broadened into a furious assault on inadequate schools, unemployment, and bad housing, because Negroes sensed these were the fruits of the second-class status to which denial of civil rights had consigned them. It is the most vital social reform movement in America today, because Negroes suffer most from inadequate schools, unemployment, bad housing, and the ravages of automation. But before it runs its full course and reaches its goals, it will have to become a component of a larger social reform movement. Fair employment will not become full reality without full employment; fair housing will not fulfill the Negroes' dream unless the housing supply is expanded; integrated schools will not prove satisfactory until the American school system integrates its graduates into a society that has faced and solved the problems bred by automation; the Negro cannot escape his share of poverty until poverty itself is banished. The Negro has not yet faced these larger issues; what he wants at the moment is to close the gap that yawns between him and other Americans.

The political storm that will be raised as the Negro demands realistic measures to remove racial handicaps and give him an even start will shake the nation, just as Stevens' "forty acres and a mule" proposal shook the post-Civil War South, and for the same reason: we are at crisis again.

We must choose between adherence to policies that will continue the isolation of the Negro and harden his color-caste status or devising new means that will facilitate and hasten his entrance into the mainstream of American life. Negroes will either become eligible for membership in the affluent society or the majority of them will become members of a pariah class, preyed upon and, in turn, preying upon the body politic and its social institutions. There is no royal road to reform, no petal-strewn path to progress in this situation. Handicapped Negroes, the vast majority, cannot overcome the odds against them by having the burden lifted off their backs with the bidding to run a race, starting from where they are, against equally un-burdened and swift competitors. The figurative ten-yard differential *can* be eliminated by moving them forward that distance or by hobbling the long-advantaged front runners. The latter alternative is socially wasteful and unthinkable. What remains is today's necessity for pref-erential assistance for kept-laggard Negroes—the undoing of a century of wrongdoing.

II

DOROTHY KENYON

What We Face Today

The revolution, of course, has been a long time brewing, and has been hovering on the horizon for centuries. It was latent in our first Revolution when the defect of a slave society in a free land was carried over into and embedded in our Constitution. Our treasured Bill of Rights omitted slaves altogether. And this pattern has persisted (in Mississippi and parts of Alabama and Georgia, for instance) down to the present day. Habits and customs have been built up around this economic anachronism of plantation slave-type labor; and the resultant attitude of white supremacy, which is very contagious, has spread

Dorothy Kenyon, a former Judge of the Municipal Court of New York City, is Chairman of the Equality Committee of the American Civil Liberties Union.

far beyond the South. The pattern is one of exclusion of Negroes from the main streams of culture—educational, political, economic, and social—as though they were, at best, subhuman. Even Jefferson, who pondered deeply and sympathetically the plight of the Negro, suggested that tests be made to see if he had a human brain, if he were in truth educable. Who has not heard others occasionally say almost the same thing today, but without Jefferson's sympathy?

The Civil War was our first mass uprising of conscience. But it was motivated by other forces too—a clash of economic cultures, growing Federal strength embodied in the concept of unity versus States' rights, a power struggle between North and South, and so on. All of this confused the issues and diminished the significance of slavery as the critical one. The result, in terms of human freedom, was a muddle. Human beings were freed from physical bondage, but left pitifully poor, "abject and ignorant . . . mere children," as was said in *Strauder* v. *West Virginia*, in 1879,* to make their way toward independence as best they could with little help, even from their friends, in the South or in the North.

---

* 100 U.S. 303, decided in 1879. One of the earliest cases under the Fourteenth Amendment. It also spoke of the "habitual . . . discriminations" which had been visited upon him "as an inferior and subject race," of "such gross injustice and hardship" as to constitute "practically a brand upon him," and the "jealousy and positive dislike" which many felt for Negroes and the "race prejudice" which was already developing against them. The opinion, although almost one hundred years old, has a painfully modern ring.

To help him in his upward struggle there were enacted in quick succession three amendments: the Thirteenth, abolishing slavery as such; the Fourteenth, extending the prohibitions of the Bill of Rights to the states, thereby including Negroes in its protections; and the Fifteenth, extending to him the right to vote. Congress also passed broadly based civil rights laws but these were soon robbed of their efficacy by the decision in the *Slaughter House* cases* which declared them unconstitutional insofar as the prohibited discriminations went beyond acts of government and were acts of private individuals instead. This decision effectively barred any legal protection against private discrimination (except that which individual states might provide) in many areas of ordinary living, such as transportation, housing, eating establishments, places of entertainment, and the like, unless government in some way controlled or participated in such projects. This was a great setback in the Negro's fight for freedom and was directly responsible for most of the Jim Crow segregation laws that quickly followed. What civil rights laws there were after that were mostly confined to the Northern states, and even there for many years they were honored more in the breach than in the observance.

In fact, one of the more disturbing phenomena of the times has been the speed and intensity with which the insidious philosophy of white supremacy has spread and taken root even in the North, like poison ivy running riot over the land, often without our even being aware of its

---

* 16 Wall 36.

presence within and among us. Some of it was probably there already, but proximity to the South didn't help. The contagion has gone even further and at times has seemed to have permeated the ranks of Negroes themselves, as though they were hypnotized into accepting for themselves the stereotype image created for them by white people. I am reminded of a terrible book called *The Man Who Laughed*, the tale of a man whose face had been carved by torture into a hideous distorted perpetual smile while within him his heart was breaking. In a sense this story is akin to the remark of the tragic Negro mother who, when the white overlord who employed her as a sharecropper came to ask if she were going to send her child to the newly integrated school on the following Monday as provided for by the court order, answered with dignity, "I know my place." And the child did not go to the integrated school the next Monday. The torture that led her to her reply was the thought of starvation or worse for her children. She doubtless prayed as she spoke. So the scorn of Negroes for "Uncle Toms" seems to me not quite justified in all circumstances. In my own mind, his image is closer to that of the man who laughed.

Now we have moved into the twentieth century and are already two-thirds of the way through it, the century of social revolution, for women, for slaves, for minority groups everywhere. Since World War II the pace has quickened as Gunnar Myrdal predicted it would. And now suddenly the dogs of Birmingham have bayed their warning, Harlem has rioted against the police, and the hurricane is upon us. We know that we can drift (or remain "uninvolved," to quote the latest word in the new vocabulary) no longer. This storm is our storm, the storm of human beings crying for fair play everywhere, and we cannot stand aside. We must move with the wind. And yet, as part and parcel of the society that is being challenged, many of us laden with habits and customs of white supremacy we are only dimly aware of, what can we do?

What We Are After

"Fundamental freedoms for all, without distinction as to race, sex, language or religion." "Human rights and human dignity." These are the words of the Charter of the United Nations, put into that document at the last moment when the dignitaries, gathered in San Francisco to sign it, began to realize that the peace and security for which the blueprint of a United Nations had been designed was not enough—that peace itself is not enough—unless there be freedom too. And so civil liberties for all mankind were included (almost as an afterthought) as an integral part of the Charter.

The battle for individual freedom, as we know, is nothing new in the world, any more than it is in the United States. But its sudden expansion at the end of World War II to encompass everybody everywhere has had an electrifying effect. Women have been given the vote almost everywhere. Saudi Arabia with its slave populations, South Africa with its subjugated "natives" and "coloreds," the United States with its Deep South heritage of slavery and a freer North in juxtaposition, and other countries everywhere have all been stirred to their depths. The coming of great change in these areas is nowhere disputed. The only questions are how far and how fast? And (with side glances at South Africa and parts of our own Deep South), how peacefully?

In exploring this world problem of many facets we in the United States must first consider how best to proceed in view of all our special circumstances and problems, since proceed we must and, apparently, on all fronts at once. The Negro in the United States has been discriminated against in all areas. He needs a better education; more economic opportunities; a chance to play his part as a citizen, to vote, hold public office, serve on juries and in all other governmental capacities; to enjoy all governmental benefits, such as social security, farm and labor benefits and the like, as well as all intellectual and cultural advantages; in short, to mingle and participate freely in the life of his times just like anybody else, white, black, or what have you, and without discrimination anywhere. What we have to do is to discover the best methods of opening these various doors of opportunity to him. Can it be done wholly by legal or political, or even social, means, or should moral or religious influences be used as well? There is strong religious motivation in this country for Negro rights, as symbolized in the words "brotherhood," "breaking of bread together," and the like. How can public opinion be gauged in this area of our thinking?

What are people's attitudes on the subject? What can be done about modifying them, if they are hostile? How can they be best mobilized to bring about results?

It comes down to a question of attitudes. For, in the last analysis, it is human attitudes that promote or stand in the way of change. Many people think that if we have a problem we pass a law, and presto! the problem is solved. But, in the words of the song, "It ain't necessarily so," or even very likely. Not, at least, if too few people are prepared for it or too many dislike it. Look at the prohibition law, for instance, a famous example of a law that was nullified to death because of adverse public reaction. A law can be tinkered with, changed here or added to there, perhaps, to effect improvements. But if the public is not ripe for the change, such gains will be insignificant.

So let us start at the heart of the matter, the attitudes of people, what they instinctively feel about things, why they feel that way, their habits of thinking, and what they are thinking about. Right now we can be sure that Negroes play a prominent part in the thinking of white people. That part of their thinking is therefore a part of the problem; it is what white people have to try to understand, the emotional hurdle they have to get over before America can hope to work out appropriate changes in law and custom that will stick.

There seems to me to be certain helpful guidelines that we can lay out for ourselves in this work all of us must do. Although at first glance they may seem academic, perhaps, and the institutions involved rather remote from our theme, the institutions themselves are nevertheless extraordinarily close to—and, in fact, extremely sensitive to—the changing attitudes of people, upon which, in fact, they depend for their power. I suggest first, therefore, a brief look at the nature of habits and customs, how they develop in themselves and how they relate to the development of law and order as we understand the terms, and their interplay and interaction each upon the other. Then I would consider the scope of civil liberties under our constitutional pattern as developed by the decisions of the Supreme Court and the specific role of our Bill of Rights, in the areas both of substantive rights as such and of their enforcement—a right without a remedy being, as every Negro knows, a futile thing. We should then consider the extent not only of negative, but of affirmative (mandatory) enforcement techniques, particularly of court decisions. Next, we should take a quick look at the role of public opinion in support of or opposition to the Supreme Court in all these matters. With this background we will be ready to discuss a variety of different methods of achieving equality of opportunity for Negroes and the meaning of some of the terms employed to describe those methods, among them such controversial words as "quotas," "preferential treatment," "compensatory treatment," "color blindness," "neighborhood schools," "bussing," even "equality" itself. Finally, I would hope that all this may reveal to us some good methods for achieving equality and fair play for all. This is quite an undertaking, admittedly; impossible, perhaps; but, in our search for light in the confused darkness of our present problems, at least worth trying.

Habits and Customs: Their Crystallization into Law and Their Interplay Thereafter

The smallest grouping of people must have rules whereby it governs itself and its constituent members. A single individual can possibly live as he pleases. But once he combines with others, generally for greater safety as well as companionship, he quickly learns that there must be rules of "live and let live" if such a group is to have tolerable interrelationships. So rules are adopted to curb the more obvious forms of antisocial conduct. Later, leadership develops and the strong tend to dominate the weak. The rules reflect that situation too. If oppression becomes too great, a reaction may set in and the rules be modified or changed. Eventually, a fairly stable society may emerge on the basis of a sort of balance between these contending forces. Whatever their origins or nature, these rules of conduct in a relatively stable society tend to develop and harden into customs, and then, through repetition, into habits of living and thinking. Frequently, as time goes on, they develop such tenacity and emotional power as to continue to exist long after the reasons for their adoption in the first place have disappeared, been forgotten, or even become no longer valid or desirable. People's thoughts tend to become conditioned by these habits; the things they have always heard tend to be the things they know and believe in; reiteration gives familiarity and strength to the idea; a new (because strange) idea often becomes more or less suspect. In fact, habits and customs (often unbeknownst to us) can be the real tyrants in our lives, if we do not watch our step.

Law begins as crystallization of custom. It constitutes the rules of conduct among individuals in a society, rules that were originally passed on in primitive society by word of mouth but which, as society becomes more sophisticated, are eventually reduced to writing and receive the stamp of approval as laws by those in power.

New laws, like changes in custom and habit, come about because of changing circumstances and interests and viewpoints in the world around us. New activities develop, new ideas are expressed, and soon, if interest is aroused, new laws relating to them are likely to appear on the statute books. Thus laws are created, molded, and changed as circumstances and public interest dictate. They generally lag after customs and changes in public viewpoint, being as a rule the reflection and recognition in much more minute detail and in more permanent form of these informal strictures.

The reasons behind some of these rules of law, like the habits and customs from which they derive, are also sometimes forgotten or become no longer valid; yet the law itself frequently lingers on. That was the case with the Common Law in England; finally, the only way to get rid of it was to invent a new rule called Equity—less technical, more practical, and more compassionate to weak individuals than the old law. The Common Law remained to wither on the vine (a good British compromise) and it is still withering away briskly (the British are not only good compromisers but are also famous for the tenacity of their habits; they still carry bouquets of flowers to their courthouses, although the open sewers in the streets, the cause of this quaint custom, were covered over centuries ago). Our Blue Laws are another illustration of neglect through obsolescence.

Laws are passed to be obeyed, but it doesn't always happen that way, as we have seen from our extraordinary experience with the prohibition laws as well. But generally the passage of a law is in response to a substantial enough demand from the articulate public that it is likely to stick, for a while at least. If opinion is divided, of course, there may be trouble for a time. The Civil Rights Act is definitely wanted by a substantial majority of the people of the United States. But in certain areas the articulate public is almost solidly against it and it has already run into some trouble. The extent of the trouble will turn upon the extent to which habits and customs have played upon and indoctrinated these people and how much they will be guided by them, as distinguished from the effect on them of arguments from other people, nearby and elsewhere, in conflict with them on the merits or morality or practicalities of the case.

Hence we see a close relationship between the habits of mind and attitudes that help to determine peoples' thinking and the laws that people enact. There is a continual interplay between the two.

As Elihu Root once remarked (and I can only paraphrase his wonderfully lucid prose), laws projected into the world rarely take effect precisely as the wording would lead you to expect. No matter how carefully a law is drafted, the impact of the living world upon it, with its habits of centuries—perhaps counter to that law—and the differing attitudes of people with all their complexities and variety, is profound. The direction of the law is actually compounded of these two factors: the law's text, meaning, and intent on the one hand; and the facts of contemporary life on the other, resulting not in the straight line of the law but in a line deflected to the extent that the outside forces are powerful enough to do so. Depending on the strength of these outside forces the laws are shaped, interpreted, warped, cut down, or even nullified accordingly.

We have seen the extreme illustration of total defeat of the prohibition laws, of obsolescence resulting in neglect of the Blue Laws, and so on. Even the Thirteenth, Fourteenth, and Fifteenth amendments, part of the Constitution though they be, were pretty effectively watered down for many years, and the Fourteenth has only recently begun to come into its own. But the most interesting illustration for us now is the Civil Rights Act itself, which has been in the making for a number of years, has the vigorous backing of a large segment of the population, and yet has been enforced with difficulty or not at all in

various areas where there is a large body of strong local opposition. The final outcome of these conflicts of pressures is not yet. Much hangs in the balance. But no one can deny the power of public opinion and no one can claim that laws alone, without public conviction of their need, can solve our burning problem.

Laws alone are obviously not enough. They are often even, as Chief Justice Warren has recently observed, too little and too late. "The law is slow to move," he said, "it has waited for problems to develop and then belatedly sought to make rules for solving them." So law is not the perfect weapon to our hands.

But there is another side to the coin in this interplay of law and custom. For just as law is influenced and deflected off course at times by strongly entrenched opposing habits and customs, so it in turn can and does influence and deflect those same habits and customs. Scores of laws have been accepted—with enthusiasm by some, with utmost reluctance by others, but eventually accepted—with the result that the opposing habits are gradually forgotten and new habits formed in their stead, often as a direct consequence of the law's existence. This is what we must hope will happen in the case of our new Civil Rights Act.

The laws we are talking about here are the laws enacted nowadays in legislative bodies (congresses, state legislatures, parliaments, and the like) made up of elected representatives of people in a democracy. Other laws, by order or decree of the executive (in less democratic countries), are not quite so directly responsive to the people; but in the long run they, too, are likely to stand or fall on the basis of public approval.

Our Constitution and the Bill of Rights

But there is another kind of law, which is not so responsive to public pressures and is therefore not quite so fluid or so easily upset. This is a good thing since, as we can readily see, great fluidity can at times be highly undesirable—if not fatal—to democracy as we know and want it. Public opinion is capable of wild fluctuations and can go to great extremes as the segregationists, such as the Wallaceites and others of their way of thinking, have proven. Germany was once swept by powerful public pressures into Nazism, Fascism, murder, and worse. The rule of the majority may at times ride roughshod over the rights of helpless people, weak minorities. And Negroes are, of course, and always have been a minority in our population.

That is exactly where civil rights and civil liberties come in. These are the rights of human beings, individual human rights, rights that are regarded as so precious to every individual that no king, emperor, tyrant, conqueror, or even a majority in a democracy can be allowed to take them away. Of course, rights, no matter how precious, can always be taken away by force and violence. But this is brute force, not law and order.

The rights we are speaking of are protections against government itself. By spelling them out in our Constitution and pledging government to support them, we put them beyond the range of ordinary legislation and the will of the majority.

Constitutions develop out of society's need for law and order coupled with adequate protection for individual rights. Where men join together in a society and leadership develops, the strong, as we know, tend to dominate the weak. But the instinct of freedom is a hardy plant in almost every breast and it quickly sets to work to redress the balance. The result is a struggle, familiar in almost every society, between tyranny and freedom, the freedom-lovers claiming that authority, which gives physical protection, should protect the interests of individual liberty as well, even against itself. "Life, liberty and the pursuit of happiness," Jefferson said, "are our God-given rights," "and to secure those rights" men place themselves under government.

The Constitution guarantees our freedoms; that is what it was designed to do, it was one part of its reason for being. And the Supreme Court, as watchdog of our liberties under the Constitution, defends us even from the inroads of government itself upon them.

I might say a word at this point about the meaning of the words "rights," "liberties," "freedoms," "civil rights," and "civil liberties," which I have so far used almost interchangeably. That is because, in my judgment, there are and should be no differences among them. "Civil rights" and "civil liberties," in particular, are one and the same. There is no logical difference at all between them. The

reason for the distinction sometimes made, it has been suggested, is that the "liberty" vaunted so highly by Jefferson
and proclaimed by him to be God-given was an attribute
of free men, not of slaves. So when Negroes became free
it seemed somehow unfitting to bestow upon them the
same triumphant God-given epithet. The slave, so recently freed, was a suppliant for the rights that go with
freedom. Thus, the term "rights" was used in a sense as a
status symbol and as a subtle reminder of his former inferiority. But all the liberties and freedoms guaranteed by
our Bill of Rights are rightfully his; and in speaking of
them in future, by whichever term, I shall, of course, always be referring to both white and black as equally entitled to them.

These liberties of ours were a matter of great concern
to our Founding Fathers and to the thirteen states that
signed the Constitution. Some of the states, in fact,
thought them so important that they refused to sign the
Constitution as it originally stood or to join the Union
until the Bill of Rights had been added. And they have as
great significance for us today as they had then, because
they all represent the fruits of battles against tyranny and
oppression, all fought by individuals, often against great
odds. No freedoms are ever won without a struggle and
eternal vigilance is the price we pay for keeping them. So
the Fathers were right in insisting that what they considered the most essential of them must go into the Constitution.

The first of these, the right of religious freedom, of free

speech, free press, free association, demonstrations in support of grievances, and all the things that go with them; the right to think freely and to say what one thinks; the right to dissent, to seek the truth, as the scholar must, and to follow it no matter where it may lead—this great bundle of rights arose out of the religious battles and persecutions of the Middle Ages and is in essence a religious concept. In fact, the right to the free exercise of religion is the first in point of time, and perhaps the mightiest, of our freedoms. Out of these early religious persecutions also grew that clause in the Fifth Amendment that a man cannot be compelled to bear witness against himself which has been so frequently misunderstood and has caused such endless discussion in recent years.

Next is the great principle known as the "law of the land," the concept, of English origin, that there is a law above the king, an unwritten law before which even the all-powerful king must bow. This "law of the land" is nothing more or less than an expression of the impulse of fair play, our old friend due process of law. It includes such things as the right to trial by a jury of one's peers (as distinguished from the judge, who was in those days only the king's man), to know the nature of the charge against one, to be represented by counsel, to have the right of habeas corpus, and so on, through all the intricacies of court procedures as we know them today, all basically founded on the principle of the Golden Rule, the rule of fair play. An increasingly important adjunct of this right is the right to privacy, originally expressed through the old maxim that an Englishman's home is his castle, before entering which even the king must knock. In modern democratic parlance this means the policeman (or a tapped telephone wire, or a concealed microphone), who cannot enter without a warrant based on reasonable cause and is limited in subject matter to the matter in hand (i.e., not with a general warrant as the Constitution describes it, or, in homelier language, not on a "fishing expedition").

And finally comes the principle of equality, of which I shall say nothing here because, as we know, the Founding Fathers omitted slaves from the Constitution and equality in consequence means something quite different nowadays from what it meant then.

It is significant, and I think worthy of special mention, that all of these civil liberties principles have a strong religious tinge and that religion gave them their first impetus.

More interesting, however, than the things included in the original Constitution and its amendments (which are old hat to most of us until somebody tries to take them away) are the things left out of the Constitution which seem important today. Life was a lot simpler in the agrarian slave society of Jefferson's time and we have lived and learned a great deal since then. Most of the differences between now and then do not relate primarily to Negroes' problems but apply to all of us alike in the process of development of our economy and our concepts of democracy. I can only speak briefly of a few of them here.

First of all, democracy, we have now come to believe, must rest upon the base of universal adult suffrage (with a dash of literacy perhaps thrown in), which we certainly did not dream of in Revolutionary days. And voting rights for all in turn presupposes and virtually requires literacy for all, the ability at least to read and write, if there is to be any democratic meaning to the use of the secret ballot or any intelligent voting by the voter. And that, in turn, presupposes free public education, a basic minimum for everybody.

Neither of these matters was touched upon, understandably enough, in our original Constitution. Large segments of our population were not even thought of then as citizens, much less voters, among those left out of consideration being slaves and women. Voting itself was still considered something of a privilege and was limited to property owners. As for education, it was never thought of as having any universal application at all, certainly not as a responsibility of government. It was thought of solely as a rich man's privilege.

I might add that the right to vote has never been guaranteed by the Constitution except as it is implied in our form of representative government and the clauses relating to election procedures, one of which, for representative apportionment purposes, values a slave as three-fifths of a man. The only guarantee is "a Republican form of government" "for every state." The decisions in the legislative apportionment cases of the Supreme Court in recent years might perhaps be considered a small step in this direction insofar as they were decided under the Equality Clause of the Fourteenth Amendment, which was held to ensure equal voting rights for all, as well as the Fifteenth and Nineteenth amendments.

Neither is the right to an education guaranteed by or even mentioned in the Constitution, unless the Brown decision in 1954 overruling the "separate but equal" doctrine of *Plessy* v. *Ferguson* might also be considered a small step in that direction, insofar as it was also decided under the Equality Clause. The only references to public schools as such appear in state constitutions and laws wherein public school attendance is made obligatory up to various grades and ages in every state except South Carolina. Whether we will ever go further than this in terms of any Federal guarantee of education is uncertain, although the term "illiteracy" has already attained the status of a dirty word and we may eventually come to regard it as a national disgrace and take national action accordingly.

We have come, it is true, a long way since Jefferson's time and have added other amendments, notably, the Thirteenth, Fourteenth, Fifteenth, and Nineteenth, to the Constitution. But we still have a long way to go, the longest way of all being in the area of racial discrimination which encompasses practically every phase of modern life.

This should not discourage us too much, however. For if there is one thing that every student of civil liberties must understand, it is that civil liberties is a developing concept, continually growing and expanding in our ever-changing society. The great principles—freedom of religion and expression, fair play, equality—remain the same; but the specific application of those principles must change to fit changed conditions. It is also true that we have gained in the depth of our knowledge of democracy itself since Revolutionary days and that changing times have brought new areas of freedom and new problems in their train. The rights of Negroes and other minority groups and the rights of labor, for instance, as well as individual human rights in such matters as jobs and housing have all come to the fore. Great strides have already been made in state FEPC and fair-housing laws and more will come. And the right to assemble to petition for redress of grievances, under the title of "demonstrations," has taken a tremendous lease on life and is under study for possible development in all sorts of directions.

These new matters—unfinished business and business yet to come, the difficult, delicate, elusive questions of constitutional law they inevitably raise, and the baffling questions of enforcement they all present—make up the field with which the Supreme Court must deal.

The Arm of the Constitution—the Supreme Court

Constitutional rights beyond the reach of tyrant king or legislative majority are empty if we cannot enjoy them. We need a strong enforcement arm. This we have in our

Supreme Court, a unique instrument set up under the Constitution, as supple and sensitive as any ever created, which is now more than ever on the firing line of freedom. It is rather remarkable in its set-up, being the highest court in a Federal system, binding together a large number of formerly sovereign states into a strong Federal union of delegated powers, and committed to the settlement among them of disputed questions of jurisdiction of all sorts in this complex hierarchy and bundle of interlocking rights —Federal, state, and individual. There has to be a court somewhere, an umpire so to speak, to decide all disputed matters, and in the process guard our freedoms, if we are to have a government of law and not of anarchy, and also of free men. And the logical place to have it is certainly at the top.

It is also well chosen for its task. The President chooses its nine members with great care and with the advice and consent of the Senate. They are picked not only for high quality, but also with wide geographical diversification in mind. (New York, in other words, does not dominate the scene, which may be hard on the Court's collective brains but good for the country.) The President himself is elected by popular vote, although the vote is counted by states. And senators represent all states, regardless of size, equally. So no state can complain.

All this seems good and sound and sensible. One could hardly think of a better method of choice. Furthermore, as a matter of fact, no President can ever anticipate how his candidates will turn out. Some Presidents have certainly been surprised, but that is the human gamble in every such situation and, since we Americans love a gamble, that is also all to the good. The system and set-up would seem to be about as fair as one could ask for; the caliber of the judges is of the highest. The Court has a splendid record of accomplishments (with a few ups and downs, the Brown and the Dred Scott cases for illustrations of each) behind it.

And it is a powerful court, make no mistake about that. Just as the Constitution of the United States is the law of the land, so the decisions of the Supreme Court, in interpreting it, are equally the law of the land.

Mr. Justice Frankfurter, in one of the Little Rock cases, reminded us of this. Referring to the notable early case of *Marbury* v. *Madison*, decided in 1803, he said: "This decision declared the basic principle that the Federal judiciary is supreme in the exposition of the law of the Constitution, and that principle has ever since been respected by this court and the country as a permanent and indispensable feature of our constitutional system."

And Mr. Chief Justice Hughes (in slightly tarter language, because he was dissenting at that point) said: "The Constitution is what the Supreme Court says it is."

Our Constitution and the civil liberties it guarantees have indeed a stalwart and powerful champion in the Supreme Court. In the last two decades it has made decisions of extraordinary significance in the field of human freedoms. The list of its decisions in support of civil liberties grows apace until now, while the Court is in session,

they have become almost required weekly reading in the
New York Times. Twenty or so years ago a superb
group of Negro lawyers began to bring case after case
in important fields before them and won almost every
case. Among these were primary and voting rights cases
in the political field, jury discrimination cases in the field
of justice, a restrictive covenant case in the field of private
housing, and the great school desegregation cases (*Brown
v. Board of Education*) declaring the doctrine of "separate
but equal" schooling fallacious and unconstitutional. This
last case brought in its train a whole host of other types of
cases, such as equal use of public accommodations and of
interstate transportation, restaurants, and related facilities.
There has also been a flood of cases implementing the
school desegregation decisions; and in the last few years
an increasing number relating to equal rights in private
accommodations (the famous sit-in cases). The Court has
gone the whole way in acceptance of the principles of full
equality. The difficulties, as usual, lie in the area of their
application. Granting the existence of these eloquently
expressed principles, how can we enforce them?

*Enforcement Procedures; Negative and
Affirmative (Mandatory) Decrees;
Affirmative Obligations of Government*

In implementing their decisions courts issue them in
appropriate cases in the form of injunctions, negative or
affirmative (mandatory), as the case may require. A nega-

tive injunction, for instance—and most of them generally are negative—is much like a "cease and desist" type of order, telling the defendant to stop doing the thing the court has found objectionable. Most cases lend themselves to this type of order more readily than to a positive command, since they are easier both for the individual to obey and for the court to supervise. It is always easier to stop doing something one has been doing than to begin doing something new; and as far as the court is concerned the prohibited act is generally clearly defined and the obedience easy to identify. But there is no reason why the court should not issue an affirmative (i.e., mandatory) order if it considers such desirable, and sometimes it cannot get the kind of compliance it needs unless it does. But it tends to do so reluctantly, the reason being obvious, namely, that it is difficult to formulate a command to act and hard to decide whether it has been properly obeyed or not. It is one thing to say "Stop; what you are doing is bad" and quite another (quite an intellectual exercise, in fact) to say "Be good instead of bad; do so-and-so." Hence the easy way is just to say "Stop."

In civil liberties cases it has been traditional to use negative injunctions almost entirely. There is a good historical reason why this should be so and why mandatory injunctions have so rarely been used in civil liberties cases in the past: these cases were originally concerned, and solely concerned, with prohibitions against the king. Civil liberties began as curbs on the power of the king. There were certain things that not even the king could do: he could not interfere with people's right to speak, nor tamper with the court rules of due process, nor enter a man's house if he had not knocked and received permission. These were our classical civil liberties and all were curbs on the king's power to act; they were stop signs against him, a negative command. But as our concepts of civil liberties have expanded and democratic government by majority rule has taken the place of the king, the idea has been gradually developing that government is not only obligated not to deprive us of these precious individual rights of ours but actually has an affirmative responsibility to help us in their preservation.

This was illustrated in rather exaggerated form in the early days of the United Nations Commission on Human Rights, when it started work on a Declaration of Human Rights and a proposal was made to put it all into legally binding "multilateral treaty" form, with the enforcement provisions usual in such a covenant. All of the classical civil liberties, the ones in the Bill of Rights and prohibitory in nature, were there. But many other rights were there as well, many of them representing no more than the unrealized goals and aspirations for the future of an ideal democratic state, neither sharply enough defined nor sufficiently realized in fact and law to constitute the material for a binding legal obligation. For along with the rights of free speech, due process, equality, and so on, other things were listed: the right to work, to a decent standard of living, decent housing, security in old age, cultural opportunities, and the like, along with the right to vote and to an education—all fine things, but most of them (except for voting and education) much too generalized and visionary for any formal legal document. It was quickly realized that not all such matters could be put into an enforcible covenant with legal penalties for violation. So the document was divided into two parts, one consisting of the classic civil liberties in covenant form, with penalties for their violation, the other consisting of a Declaration combining all human rights, both those already achieved in law and those constituting the hopes and aspirations for democracy in future.

This is significant insofar as it points up the gradual change from the conception of mere prohibitions in defense of civil liberties of the early days to an increasing awareness of the need to impose affirmative responsibilities on government in their active defense today. And this idea keeps growing on us and manifesting itself in a great variety of different ways as the plight of the Negro in respect to basic liberties in this country becomes better known and recognized for what it is—his massive rejection by and exclusion from the warp and woof of white people's lives.

This idea of the need for positive affirmative action by government in defense of equality of civil liberties, however, actually goes back a long way in our history. In 1879, in *Strauder* v. *West Virginia*, involving discrimination through exclusion of Negroes from juries under the Fourteenth Amendment, the Court said:

The words of the Amendment, it is true, are prohibitory, but they contain a necessary implication of a positive immunity, or right most valuable to the colored race—the right to exemption from legal discriminations, implying inferiority in civil society, lessening the security of their enjoyment of the rights which others enjoy, and discriminations which are steps toward reducing them to the condition of a subject race.

More recent Federal cases on the same theme have been even more explicit. One case described the jury commissioners who select juries as being charged with "a positive affirmative duty" to make a fair sampling of all the distinctive groupings in their communities so as to achieve a representative cross-section for their jury lists; and it is made clear that this means much more than a negative obligation not to discriminate. This is not to say that this theory, while splendid, has yet been put into practice, particularly in the state courts of the Deep South, where Negroes have always been excluded from all but token participation in the judicial machinery. But it is a hopeful portent for the future.

But, if jury service is important, voting rights are probably even more so. And here, too, we see increasing indications of the government's assumption of major affirmative action in support of this right. One of its latest efforts has been in the field of voter registration, where it has sought to ensure fairness in the giving of literacy tests and has entered the courts actively as plaintiff in behalf of voting rights, the 1957 Civil Rights Act having given the government itself that right. Previously the aggrieved

Negro was the only one who could bring such a suit in his own behalf. We may also see Federal Registrars set up some day as a safeguard of voting rights.

Expanding on this practice, the government has now obtained a similar power to initiate actions under various sections of the new Civil Rights Act of 1964, including public accommodations and public facilities. Suits started by the government are already under way to test that law's constitutionality and cases of various sorts are anticipated. Recent equal pay laws are another illustration of government suits to protect the rights of female workers.

These same ideas are also spreading in the states. The local Commissions on Human Rights and the local FEPC committees are thinking in terms of the same kind of government help in initiating suits in behalf of those discriminated against—in the fields of housing or employment, as the case may be—instead of leaving the burden and expense of litigation entirely to the Negro. Legislation to that effect is being sought in various states.

All these things show a growing appreciation of the need to have government assume affirmative responsibility for assuring these rights to its citizens.

The same idea, of imposing affirmative responsibility on government, is also being carried out but by a slightly different technique in the field of education, where as in the other cases there is no affirmative right to an education as such but only to *equal* education. The Brown school desegregation cases, for instance, are an illustration of what can be done by use of the mandatory injunction. The mandatory injunction itself is worth looking into, therefore, to see just what it can do and is doing in this field.

There are many more civil liberties cases nowadays than there used to be where mandatory injunctions are employed, and in most of these cases nothing else will do. This is true of the legislative apportionment cases where the Court's mandatory orders in effect say "Stop, and do something better; if the something better is not spelled out to our satisfaction, then we (the Court) may have to formulate our own apportionment scheme for you." The difficulties involved in doing this are obvious and may have had something to do with public reaction to the decisions, although the people who have attacked the Court on these decisions are mainly people who wish to take jurisdiction over such matters away from the Federal courts and keep it in the hands of the states. But, difficult as they are, these mandatory procedures are essential in this type of case. And the retention of jurisdiction in the Federal courts over cases involving equality of voting rights is vital to our civil liberties.

Mandatory injunctions can also be very important at times by making enforcement possible where a negative decree might have no practical results at all. This has certainly proved true in the Brown and other school desegregation cases where the mandatory injunction has been the only thing that has in many cases kept the decree from becoming a dead letter in the face of solid opposition. (Take Mississippi for illustration—after ten years, in the fall of 1964, it got started on integration with a handful of Negro pupils.) To tell the truth, the ordinary negative injunction, the order to halt, means very little if you do not know what you are expected to do in its place. If you are to stop discriminating, you must do something else. But what? You have plenty of excuses for doing something grossly inadequate or for not trying at all if nobody gives you a hint as to what will suffice. And what will suffice? Obviously, in these cases, nothing short of desegregation or integration (if there be a difference) with all deliberate speed. So the Court has to spell out, in specific language, what has to be done. And when it does, the thing is done; otherwise, not.

If the segregation is not intentional but the result, let us say, of segregated housing, for which the particular school is not responsible, there then arises the question whether that school can persist in its discriminatory posture or whether there is some affirmative duty on it to desegregate or integrate, once the discrimination, though unintentional at the outset, has been called to its attention. The Brown cases, covering only intentional segregation, did not cover this point. The point has yet to be decided by the Court.

There is certainly ample legal precedent for mandatory injunctions where the Court feels it proper to issue them. And there is also precedent, as we have seen, for imposing an obligation upon those who have governmental responsibility and are in a position to do something positive to stop discrimination by affirmative acts in support of whatever civil liberties are involved. To establish equality in education under this theory, government must do more than just stop discriminating; it must initiate active steps on the road to integration. And that is precisely what the Brown cases told it to do.

In the second opinion in *Brown* v. *Board of Education* (1955), relating to the question of what decrees the Court would issue—the first decision (made in 1954) having related solely to the principle that "separate" schools were not "equal" and the intervening year having been spent in collecting additional facts in respect to conditions in the various schools concerned—the Court made clear that it would not just issue a flat prohibitory decree against discrimination, but would issue positive, affirmative proposals for the guidance of the schools as to what should be done to achieve desegregation. The cases were remanded to the local courts because of their proximity to and better knowledge of local conditions. The Supreme Court said:

The courts may consider problems related to administration . . . the school transportation system, personnel, revision of school districts and attendance areas into compact units, to achieve a system of determining admission to the public schools on a non-racial basis. . . . They will also consider the adequacy of any plans the defendants may propose to meet these problems and to effectuate a transition to a racially non-discriminatory school system. During this period of transition, the courts will retain jurisdiction. . . .

Nothing could be further from a bare negative prohibition nor more positive, affirmative, and mandatory in character than this opinion and the local decrees that followed in the various areas. By the phrase "transition to a

71

racially non-discriminatory school system," until which time the Court would not surrender jurisdiction of the case, the Court made clear its intention to see the job through until desegregation was achieved and also to place squarely upon the shoulders of the school authorities the positive, affirmative obligation to desegregate—which, in plain English, means substantial integration. Or at least I think it does.

This procedure of placing affirmative obligations on public officials and standing by to see that they carry them out may be difficult, slow, and clumsy for a court to follow. But it may be the only way to achieve enforcement in the face of open hostility such as exists in parts of the Deep South today. It works (at least it has so far) and that is the essential. This brings us back once more to the Court and the question of public attitudes.

The Supreme Court and Public Attitudes

I have said that the Supreme Court is a powerful court, the umpire of all these vital questions of civil liberties for all. And yet here in these very education cases we find it hamstrung, with one of its greatest decisions not yet fully obeyed after ten years of hard work and patient waiting. It will presumably win eventually as people gradually become resigned to new ways they previously hated and give up the struggle. But then again it may not, and there may be tragedy. What is the reason for this and what can we do to help? For the powerful Supreme Court is the watchdog of our liberties and we cannot let it go down to defeat.

It is well to remember that antagonism and resistance to some of its decisions is nothing new in the life of the Court. From the very beginning it has been in hot water. For a court of seeming tremendous power it actually has no sanctions. Almost from its first case, involving a dispute to which a state was party, it has not known how its decisions would be received or even whether its decrees would be obeyed. In those first cases, the Court often held its breath while its marshal clop-clopped on horseback all the way from Washington, D.C., to the state in question to serve the Court's decree on its governor. Would he obey? The Court, as Mr. Justice Frankfurter has said, has no power either of the sword or of the purse; it has no army at its back to enforce its decrees, only the power of prestige, of moral suasion, together with public opinion (and it had precious little of that at that time) behind it. The Court waited. The marshal arrived, rode up to the governor's mansion, handed the paper to the governor. The governor took it, he obeyed its mandate. The Court breathed again. It had been upheld as a going concern, with moral force its only effective weapon.

This has not been invariably true, of course. One recent governor has refused to obey—or made the gesture of refusing, at any rate, and then stepped aside.

The Court is older now; it has great prestige and we as a people believe in the rule of law. Yet the same thing is still true. Public opinion, not Federal troops, uphold the

Court's decisions. No wonder, then, that, as rumored, whenever it has done anything unusually daring, the Court anxiously reads the *New York Times* the next morning.

The truth is that the Court is a most unusual institution, almost unique in the world, with power to override not only the executive but the legislative branches of government as well. In many of the democracies of the world today (Great Britain, for example) the legislature, not the Court, is supreme. But not so in our country. No wonder the judges worry over the truly awful impact of their decisions, for their power, curbed as it is, is still vast. Yet they must exercise that power, for if they did not do so, the Bill of Rights itself might be jeopardized. The Court is our only sure weapon to enforce our Bill of Rights, which without it would be worthless indeed.

So the Supreme Court must tread boldly, in defense of minority and individual civil rights, yet never forgetful that its enforcement power is purely moral and rests, in the last analysis, solely on the decent opinion of mankind.

We, its public, have a corresponding responsibility, therefore, to try to understand and interpret it to others. Much of the misunderstanding arising from some of its constitutional decisions is, I believe, due to the inability of the average layman to visualize its problems, to understand what it is up against in making its decisions—in applying general rules like "equal protection of the laws" or "due process," for instance, to specific cases, in trying to determine what such general terms mean in a given factual situation of complete novelty and complexity. We tend to criticize what we do not understand. But, before we criticize, we must try to understand what the Justices are trying to do. For these men have been carefully chosen and trained for their task, they are men and scholars of the highest ability and integrity, and someone, somewhere, *has* to make these crucial decisions.

As was said by the Chief Justice of the State of New Jersey, Mr. Justice Weintraub, one of the Supreme Court's most perceptive commentators, in describing its duties and responsibilities a few years ago:

> With respect to the interpretation of acts of Congress, the Supreme Court is contending with a well-known phenomenon—legislative ambiguity. I think it enough to say that, if the Court has incorrectly divined the legislative intent, correction is within the easy reach of the authors of the ambiguity.
>
> As to its work in the interpretation of the Constitution, we may, of course, readily disagree. But the disagreement should be tempered by our understanding of the inherent difficulties of the constitutional interpretive process. It would hardly be a justifiable criticism to say the Supreme Court engages in a process of evaluation and judgment. The Constitution does not offer a literal, definitive answer to the awesome problems which confront the Court.
>
> One may read the commerce clause, the due-process clause, the equal-protection clause, a thousand times and still not detect the slightest clue to the proper decision. The answer must be found elsewhere. The constitutional framework, as we all know, is a mere skeleton expression of governmental power and individual rights. The actual contours of those powers and rights must be determined in the context of changing conditions, by a process which is more

than a mere mechanical application of a constitutional phrase to a set of facts.

Where does this leave us? A powerful and a great court, working at immense problems and doing a superlative job for freedom along lines with great creative possibilities, this Court must be made use of by us to the full, for it is one of the best instruments of freedom we have. But it too has its Achilles heel. It too depends upon and could conceivably be destroyed by adverse public opinion. So once again public attitudes, public opinions, are king. It is one of our duties to see that the Court is clearly understood and appreciated for what it is by the bulk of our people.

How to Compensate for Years of Discrimination Without Counter-Discrimination

So we come back to our starting point, public attitudes. Even the Supreme Court, great and powerful as it is, and powerful weapon as it has been and continues to be in the cause of civil rights and liberties, depends upon public opinion for its very life and needs our sympathetic help and support.

But there is more to it than that.

Let me summarize the ground that we have covered. We have discussed briefly the methods—political, educational, economic, legislative, legal, and moral—for accomplishing the aims of Negro freedom. We will presumably need to use all of them at different times, in different places, and in different ways. For the problem is everywhere and every one of us must participate in one way or another. None of us can remain on the outside, "uninvolved," as people say.

We have also talked about customs and habits, which are often buried deep inside us without our knowing or understanding what they are or recognizing how dangerous they can be. We have seen how they affect and modify laws in many ways. And we have also seen that laws can equally, and often do, modify or change habits. Perhaps the most interesting developments in that area are the new Fair Housing laws which several states have adopted and where people are being literally taught overnight to change their housing patterns of segregation, entrenched for years—and like it. Another interesting example is the new Civil Rights Act, from which we had expected very little not much more than one short year ago, and which has suddenly blossomed out in many directions. Compliance with that law, with the morning dew still on it, is already spreading smoothly and quietly into many areas (omitting the hard-core areas) of the South, and new habits are developing as the old ones fade away.

We have also looked at our Bill of Rights, stronger than laws because it represents human values so precious to individuals that not even a majority in a democracy can take them away, and for which we have fought many bloody battles in the past. We have looked at these Amendments as they were at the time of the American Revolution (with all slaves omitted); we have noted briefly their growth and development since then, the point at which they have now arrived, and their capacity for further growth; and have guessed at the future, which looks not too bad.

We have also looked at the stalwart watchdog of those liberties, the Supreme Court, which has been of tremendous importance in the development of Negro rights, particularly in the last few decades, and which is a superb tool by which to expand the frontiers of liberty and give them legal backing and sanction. We have noted with pleasure how busy the Federal courts are with many freedom issues—perhaps predominantly with school integration cases right now—and have been glad to note their affirmative, constructive approach to these questions of discrimination and of how to remove their effects. We have indicated the growing tendency to impose upon government more and more the affirmative duty to defend the Negro's positive rights to jury service, voting, equal schooling, and the like, instead of just negating discrimination. We have also noted that the Supreme Court, like all human institutions, has no power beyond the support of public opinion to execute its decrees and must rely solely upon the decent opinion of mankind.

We have taken several side glances in the direction of religion and morality, which are powerful moving forces in the development of the concept of brotherhood and which can supply great emotional power to counteract the power of often hidden forces of hostile habit. In short, we find that whereas there is no final compulsion in our laws except as they may reside in our inner compulsion toward law and order, nonviolence, peace, and freedom, there is a great moral compulsion on all of us. That is what sent our young people to Mississippi (both those who came back and those who never will) and there will be more such manifestations of faith in humankind in days to come.

The public climate is favorable now to Negro rights. This is increasingly true throughout the world and is certainly true here in the United States. Most people want to help open doors of opportunity to Negroes. The hurricane, while it has almost frightened many whites to death, has actually, in my judgment, cleared the air and emboldened white people to search their minds and souls as they never did before to try to find ways to help.

Once this has been said, the great question remains: How can we develop the massive programs of rehabilitation that are required if Negroes, who have been so massively discriminated against, are to get the help they need? The fact that they have fought alone so bravely and so brilliantly all these years for their own self-improvement is the spur for the white majority to greater action on their behalf. But how, it is asked, can we open doors of opportunity in education and employment without hurting white men, how can we give the great big push to Negroes that is needed to compensate for all the years and years of deprivation they have suffered? And how can we keep white people from resenting it?

The problems in the different fields of opportunity are

so different (as are also the remedies that might be applied) that it might seem simpler to discuss them separately. But there are also certain general considerations common to all that must be mentioned. Most of those which have come under discussion recently involve the meaning of the words used to describe them. Sometimes, with the various connotations the words take on, they can be very confusing and even misleading. Thus it is wise to check once in a while to make sure we are talking about the same thing.

Words, Words

The first expression is "color blindness," a term first used in its present connection by Mr. Justice Harlan in his famous dissent in *Plessy* v. *Ferguson*. Another is "compensatory treatment," or "preferential treatment," as it is sometimes called.

One of the strong points made by the proponents of civil rights is that there should be some form of massive compensation for all the years of massive deprivation of all opportunities that has been the lot of most Negroes. They have urged not color blindness, but quite the reverse, an intensified color-consciousness until this imbalance of opportunities is in some measure redressed. They call this "compensatory treatment," and there is great merit in the idea. Logically, of course, and if we lived in a pure and perfect world, color blindness should be the order of the day. The situation we find ourselves in is very like the situation described by Elihu Root, of the law projected into a world which is not a vacuum but is full of other things, facts, and feelings, which brought to bear upon the law deflect it from its original course and shape it into something other than itself. So it would be if we imposed the rule of color blindness upon a society bristling with discriminations against color. To do so would be not to remove discriminations but to perpetuate them, to freeze the status quo. Society must remove its discriminations first, with its eyes wide open, and then, when we have achieved a sort of heavenly balance—and not until then—should we practice color blindness.

A case recently decided in New York is illustrative of this point. It dealt with a common situation nowadays, wherein a school proposed to transfer some of its pupils from hither to yon in order to achieve greater integration. The lower court ruled against it, quoting a New York statute which said: "*No person* shall be refused admission into or be excluded from any public school in the State of New York on account of race, creed, color or national origin."

This was reversed in the higher court, on the ground that, the sole purpose of the statute having been "to prevent segregation in the public schools," its use to achieve exactly the opposite result was contrary to its purpose and, if used "to defeat efforts to desegregate schools, then in the light of the Brown decisions by the Supreme Court . . . would have to be declared unconstitutional."

As for the term "compensatory treatment," it is interesting to note that we seem to have had no difficulty so far in accepting the theory of compensatory treatment in the educational field. Equality under the Fourteenth Amendment permits differential treatment, if that be needed to produce true equality. We see this happening all the time in the schools, where equality of educational opportunity requires much more to be done for the disadvantaged student (for whatever reason—mental, physical, or environmental) than for the advantaged. Remedial reading, special courses, tutoring, expert teaching—all these are given to the backward student and are not given to the more forward students, who do not need them. This is common sense, equality, and sound constitutional doctrine as well.

As Gunnar Myrdal has said:

The Public Schools move effectively to provide education for the physically handicapped, the blind, the emotionally disturbed, and no one argues that they should not do so because they are not responsible for the condition of these unfortunate children. There is no difference in principle in providing full educational opportunity for socially and economically handicapped children.

And so we see the disadvantaged child, with a poverty-stricken slum background, beginning to be recognized at school as in need of all sorts of special aids and extra help to make up for his pitifully barren home environment. In New York City, kindergartens and even pre-kindergartens are beginning to be considered (though perhaps they were not a year ago) as essential to make up to the child for his handicap and to compensate and enable him to join with other more advantaged children and move on from there, more on a par with them than he could possibly have hoped to be otherwise. If it were not for special educational advantages at the start, and later as needed, he would never be able to catch up and to keep up with the others. Generally the obstacle to this sort of thing is money rather than resistance to the idea. No one appears to question the propriety or need for it or to begrudge the extra time and effort and expense involved. We have always assumed that some children need more attention than others in order to attain approximately the same level and it has generally been given.

Compensatory treatment for Negroes in the economic world, although based upon the same reasoning, runs into more serious difficulty—namely, competition with whites. In rivalry for jobs there are possibilities of direct confrontation of whites and Negroes, and the almost certain likelihood of bad blood between them. This is dangerous, serves no practical good purpose, and should be avoided at all costs.

Another phrase, often used in this connection, is "preferential treatment." This term has a definitely discriminatory sound. When used in relation to hiring, if it involves choosing between a white or a Negro man, equally qualified—or the Negro less qualified than the white (as he probably would be in the case of a skilled job through lack of equal training opportunities)—then it is definitely discriminatory, will operate as unfairly against the white man as it has in the past against the Negro, and should not be permitted. The term, therefore, is unfortunate and should be given up.

But that does not dispose of the problem. For if it is used in the sense of "compensatory," as it often is, there is logic behind it. Something positive must be done to compensate for the Negro's disadvantaged economic position due to the accumulation of many previous discriminations against him. In any confrontation more likely than not the Negro *is* less qualified because of inferior educational opportunities, except in the area of unskilled labor. There the choice between white and black should be on the basis of merit alone, without considerations of color or other forms of favoritism. But this does not happen often. Where it is a question of skills, the Negro will lose out practically every time. Something must be done to help him overcome his massive handicap. But it should not be done by confrontation and favoritism, which must always be avoided insofar as possible. There must be other types of action.

There has been much talk of massive crash programs of school training, accelerated apprentice training programs within the unions, removal of segregated practices within those unions which bar Negroes from both training and membership in them, and the like. All of these are absolutely sound and must be done; but they are long-range programs and cannot be accomplished overnight.

There are a lot of things, however, that can be done at

once. More conscious effort should be made to find qualified Negro candidates for jobs. They are often not sought out at the places where they can most easily be found. Because of previous rebuffs they are in many instances shy in seeking jobs and therefore have to be pursued more than is realized. Potentially good material must be checked more carefully. Much greater efforts must be made, by government as well as businessmen, to find more jobs for everybody, particularly for the poverty groups to which most Negroes through deprivation definitely belong. Negroes should not be continually put in the position of having to compete against whites. Sometimes publicity devices can be utilized to call the public's attention to the problem. Take, as a small instance, President Johnson's suggestion several months ago with respect to women. He suggested the appointment of fifty women to high posts in government as a starter toward their greater participation in high policy-making posts—women being also a disadvantaged economic group. If this were discriminatory, as I have no doubt it was, nobody batted an eyelash. And it had a psychological "lift" effect that was fine. Negroes also need psychological lifts.

Government has a great role to play here, just as it has in the area of retraining great masses of untrained people, white and Negro, for the transition to automation. In fact, government responsibility in that area is the overriding responsibility which embraces the underprivileged Negro along with all other stranded groups. Business can and should do a great deal along these lines, but government alone has the resources for the kind of job that must be done and which will help to solve the Negro problem along with the other as a part of the whole.

All these things are matters of major statesmanship. But the Negro problem simply has to be faced up to and solutions found for it. Massive compensations must be found to make up for the massive economic deprivations to which Negroes have been subjected, just as we find them for the disadvantaged school children and for the same reason, so that they may have a better chance to catch up and not forever have to trail behind. The phrase "compensatory treatment" is a good phrase and states an important truth.

The color-blind principle which we have already dismissed can also lead us astray in respect to the meaning of another word—namely, "quota." Take the case of an apartment house, for instance, which it is hopefully planned to integrate. If we go at it blindfold, we may turn up with any kind of house. If we enroll too many Negroes at the outset, this fact may tend to drive away whites. In either case our original aim is frustrated. So the suggestion has been made that Negro applicants, of whom there are generally many more than whites, be held at the outset to a minimum number, i.e., that we set up an interim Negro quota, because in that way whites can be re-assured about coming in and integration is more likely to be achieved than if we went at it haphazardly.

This suggestion has produced an uproar on the part of those opposed to quotas, although they approve of the desired result. They insist that to refuse an apartment to a Negro, after the quota number has been reached, in favor of a white is to "discriminate." This sounds like the logic of the statute, passed to aid integration, which forbade school transfers on the ground of race or color even when the transfers were being made in aid of integration, thereby defeating the very purpose for which it was designed.

The reason why some people take this position is that to them the term "quota" has become a bad word. Because of the use of the term in limiting the admission of certain ethnic groups to schools and colleges, and because it had been used in that connection as a term of limitation and exclusion, the word itself has become to them synonymous with "discrimination."

But the word itself is harmless. The word "quota" is merely a mathematical term—meaning a certain proportion of some figure. The dictionary definition is "a proportional part or share." And when applied in a good cause, as here, to accomplish the desirable result of integration, it makes no sense, to my mind, to think of it as a bad word, which in itself it is not.

To get away from this unfortunate connotation this device has sometimes been described as a "benign" quota. If another word must be found for quota, we might conceivably use the word "numbers," which is a more flexible term with no connotation of limitation or exclusion attached to it.

Other words that are rapidly developing new connotations under the pressure of events are our old friends "bussing" and "neighborhood schools." These words are being actively employed right now as weapons in the battle for (and against) integration in the New York public schools and it may be some time before we can agree on a definition for them. But the problem is worth outlining, as a clear case of confusion of meanings.

The experience in New York City is also worth observing for the light it throws on the operation of public opinion and public pressure groups in the area of Negro rights and the way words can be used to convey different meanings to different people.

The New York City schools support the principle of the neighborhood school, particularly for small children. Even in a big city, where neighborhoods are not too precise, they are thought of highly. Everyone is in agreement on that. Simply stated, the phrase means that the school should be as near the child as reasonably possible.

Bussing is simply a means of getting children to school comfortably and safely where their homes exceed a certain distance from the school. It is no part of educational policy but is a purely routine device for the benefit of children living in areas where there may be no school within walking distance for them.

New York City has a serious problem in its segregated housing; thus, the effect of the principle of neighborhood schools is to produce many schools that are all white and many that are all Negro.

Integration is an essential part of good or, as the phrase

goes, quality education. A school superintendent is bound to strive for the best, and the best *must* include a genuine effort to produce as much integration as circumstances permit. Strict conformity to the neighborhood school principle would make that impossible. There is a conflict of educational policy between the two goals.

In New York City the superintendent of schools has worked out an ingenious and imaginative compromise between the two principles. It is on a very small scale and affects very few children (the bussing involved consists of ten-minute rides at most); but it is effective in the lift it gives to genuine integration.

A group has recently sprung up which strongly opposes this proposal and the group brooks no compromise. To this group neighborhood schools are sacrosanct and rank higher than integration or almost any other part of educational policy. The group also condemns bussing, talking about it as though long distances were involved, by describing it as the bussing of children from one end of the city to the other. But the essential point they are making is that everything, integration included, must give way to the neighborhood school.

Individuals in the group have gone to court on the issue several times, and plan to do so again. They are trying to get legislation enacted to outlaw the pairing of schools, compulsory bussing, etc., and they have conducted a two-day school boycott with much attendant publicity. Their strongest appeal is to the heartstrings of mothers, who are genuinely appalled at the thought of their little children being bussed all over the city by wicked men whose principal aim seems to be to keep them as far away as possible from their fine and rightful schools, as well as from home and mother.

The position of the group is that their children have a constitutional right to go to the neighborhood schools they now go to, that they have the right in perpetuity to go to the school nearest their homes, and that they cannot be forced to be bussed anywhere. When told that the bussing is a very small part of the plan, consisting of short ten-minute rides, and that the city is opposed to longer bus rides, they respond that they consider this just an opening wedge to long-distance bussing (in spite of the city's denial) and that that is what they are opposed to. A boycott in opposition to something which is not being proposed, and to which the city is as opposed as they, would seem to have passed the bounds of rationality.

Most of these parents are white, their children attend almost exclusively white schools; and their schools rate high in academic terms. They say they are not opposed to integration. But they are adamant as to the preservation of the status quo of the neighborhood schools which, if supported by law or court decision, could well destroy the hope of integration in New York City for many years. One ponders deeply about their motivations. The movement is clearly a manifestation of the white backlash. Might some of these people be captives of habits they know not of? For certainly what they are trying to do, even if unknown to or not understood by themselves, is

to perpetuate segregation. And that spells white supremacy. It is just possible that some of them may know quite
well what they are doing. But most of them, I believe, are
genuinely confused.

The best comment I can make in this connection is to
quote some remarks recently made by Francis Keppel,
Federal Commissioner of Education:

> The common enemy remains. The enemy is segregation
> —and segregation hurts us all. Whether it be blatant in the
> South or subtle in the North, it saps and diminishes democ-
> racy and justice.
> Let us be clear about school segregation. Whether it
> exists by law or by custom, by edict or by tradition, by pat-
> terns of employment or patterns of housing, segregation
> hurts our children, Negro and white alike. And nowhere is
> this damage more devastating than in education for democ-
> racy.
> The war against segregation is a single war, but all too
> often it is waged on many flanks which are secondary to our
> objective; the elimination of racial discrimination. In educa-
> tion, these flanking skirmishes take place over neighborhood
> schools, over mobile classrooms, over compensatory educa-
> tion . . . and even over the use of a school bus.

My final word is "equality," the legal meaning of which
lies, in the last analysis, with the Supreme Court. But in
passing we may note some of its varieties. The word itself
imports no standard except as measured against something
else. There is, for instance, such a thing as the equality of
slavery; the equality of voting rights in Ethiopia where
nobody, black or white, male or female, has the right to

vote; or even the equality of opportunity to go to public school in Prince Edward County, Virginia, where all public schools, white and Negro, were abolished four years ago. There is also a thing called mathematical equality, as differentiated from something else called "actual" or "true" equality. Mathematical equality is ironically illustrated by Anatole France's quip that everybody, rich or poor, is equally free to sleep under a bridge on a snowy night. The poll or head tax is another illustration, to which may be contrasted the income tax, described as more "truly" equal because it is not based upon counting heads but upon the actual relative financial ability of each person to pay. So, too, the special treatment given the underprivileged school child might be described as mathematically unequal to the quantity of education received by the more privileged child but more "truly" equal because it gives him that boost to the general level without which he is likely to be forever handicapped—the boost being like the handicap given to even the odds in a boat race.

The equality clause of the Fourteenth Amendment is based upon this theory of differential treatment, permitting it where the differences between authentic groups are such as to make the results of differential treatment reasonably likely to produce more genuine equality than the mathematical type of identical treatment. Perhaps this doctrine (which is based upon the rule of reason) may help in the case of workers deprived of job training or job-getting opportunities, skilled or unskilled, by giving them a boost somewhere along the line as school children are boosted. In any event, it is the Supreme Court which will eventually decide all these equality questions.

And so we face the great challenge of our time. Shorn of emotion, calm and sure, and stretching our minds and imaginations to the extent we almost invariably give to the problems of war but so seldom think of giving to the problems of peace, we must advance on all fronts and at once to uproot racial prejudice. For this way only lies the American dream.

III

ROBERT L. CARTER

I

The relevance and propriety of quotas, preferences, and compensation as legitimate and rational approaches to this country's avowed goal of equality of treatment has recently become the subject of heated and extended discussion. The disputants in this controversy do not mesh into the usual ethnic, racial, and ideological alignments on the race question. Some Negro civil rights leaders and white liberals argue for preferential treatment in employment, but are opposed to all other kinds of action taken with a consciousness of race. Their colleagues dispute the wisdom and efficacy of job preferences but firmly support the use of benign quotas as the only workable method for

Robert L. Carter is General Counsel to the NAACP.

achieving an unsegregated and open housing market. Progressives and conservatives are surprised to find themselves in agreement in viewing programs of compensatory education as offering the only realistic hope of remedying the educational deficiencies of the urban Negro. Others denounce such proposals as a blind for a refusal to deal adequately and effectively with de facto school segregation. As some view it, quotas, preferences, and compensatory treatment are merely the most expeditious means to a desired and necessary end—equality of treatment— hence it is the end, not the means, that must concern us. But to others what is being advocated is discrimination— discrimination based on race, and, whatever the persuasive rationalization, its use threatens to undermine the very foundation upon which the concept of equality has been built. In sum, any discussion of these issues raises complex and perplexing problems involving moral, legal, and tactical considerations.

These concepts as race relations solutions are at war with popular, albeit superficial, understanding of the thrust of the law. We have been led to believe that the law's aim is a universal even-handedness and an impersonal color blindness. To rationalize the application of quotas or the like in an attempt to aid the Negro's drive toward equality, we are called upon to dispute the existence of legal or moral restraints to action grounded on race. We must argue that our concern is whether in purpose and effect the means employed accomplishes or perpetuates harmful discrimination on the one hand, or avoids or eliminates racial segregation on the other. If the former and the state is involved, it is constitutionally proscribed; if it is attempted through private action, morally reprehensible. Conversely, if it eliminates discrimination, it is in accord with the basic aims and purposes of the Fourteenth Amendment, civil rights statutes, and antidiscrimination laws, and in keeping with the highest standards of morality and justice.

Stanley Mosk, former Attorney General of California and now a State Supreme Court Justice, used the latter argument to answer affirmatively a question posed by the California State Board of Education—whether a school district in seeking to achieve desegregation may consider race as a factor in adopting a school attendance plan.

Although some courts have come to a contrary conclusion, their decisions have been uniformly overturned where the question raised was whether school authorities *may*, not must, take steps to desegregate. But then the contention that school attendance plans, avowedly based on racial considerations and designed to alleviate, minimize, or avoid segregation, are legally impermissible because action based on race is proscribed, could never bear close scrutiny. In the urban North segregated housing patterns are so clearly defined and so well known in the community, that common sense dictates that school authorities must know the racial composition of schools resulting from any attendance plan devised along geographical lines.

Obviously, a school board that places a school at 125th Street and 7th Avenue in Harlem, to serve the children in the immediate vicinity, must know that it has established a 100 percent Negro school. Similarly, if the board places a school on Manhattan's 82nd Street and 5th Avenue, that school will be 100 percent white. Recognition by school authorities that segregated housing exists and an open attempt by means of school placement, zoning, pairing, and other forms of school organization to create an unsegregated school system could hardly be termed legally impermissible. For by all the demands of logic, it would have to follow that the school board that creates the Harlem and 5th Avenue schools is also acting in derogation of the law.

The difference between the two situations is not that in one instance school officials are color-conscious and in the other color-blind. They are color-conscious in both cases, as they must be, if they know anything at all about their community. The difference is that in one situation color-consciousness is made to serve a desirable social, moral, and educational end (and, in the view of some, the Constitution's mandate—unsegregated education). In the other, at the very least, there is acquiescence in administrative regulations that inevitably do and must produce racial segregation and unequal educational opportunities for Negro children.

I think it is a safe prediction, despite the conflicting decisions, that attendance plans drawn with a deliberate

97

attempt to accomplish desegregation will be voided by the courts only if they are shown to be arbitrary or unreasonable, and not because they are based on racial considerations. This, of course, is a long step away from placing school boards under constitutional compulsion to desegregate—an issue with which the courts are certain to be concerned for a long time to come.

The preference and compensatory treatment thesis would appear to be conducive to a formulation that will remove any basic legal difficulties. Action based upon group status is clearly legally permissible. We have laws against child labor, to protect the right of workers to organize into labor unions, graduated income tax regulations, laws designed solely for the protection of female employees, and those giving veterans preference in public employment. These are a few examples of legislation designed to reach particular groups in the society. Certainly, in light of the Negro's disadvantaged status, laws affording him special treatment to overcome past and current disadvantages could be devised within constitutional limitations. Since approximately 50 percent of the Negro population must be classified as impoverished, general antipoverty programs, if properly administered and adequate to the task, could accomplish the same result without specific restriction to Negroes.

Yet there is nothing in the law to legally preclude as such a governmental regulation expressly designed to assist poverty-stricken Negro families. The law need not reach all of the nation's impoverished. The present Federal program most certainly cannot. Abstract symmetry is not required. So long as those similarly situated are afforded equal treatment within the reach of the regulation, no fundamental questions of legality or constitutionality are presented.

The seemingly more troublesome legal issue, however, is whether civil rights statutes do not prevent special preferences being afforded a Negro or group of Negroes as Negroes. The issue is only seemingly troublesome, because it is difficult to conceive of how such a situation could arise or be proved. Certainly, it would be difficult for courts to interpret statutes designed to eliminate discrimination against Negroes as barring an employer from hiring colored applicants on the grounds that he thereby discriminated against white persons. This would amount to a complete distortion of the reasons for the law's enactment. Conceivably, when the millennium arrives and Negroes are no longer subject to discrimination, then perhaps that case could be made. Yet, when that day does come, the fundamental question will no longer be racial discrimination. Then the black skin of the men hired and the white skin of those rejected will not be the basis upon which selection was made.

However, a number of legal questions are implicit in any quota formulation. The benign-quota concept subordinates the individual to a group interest. Experts were at one time in accord that there is in housing occupancy a point beyond which the concentration of nonwhites cannot go without causing the flight of whites. This is called the tipping point, and it has been estimated to be as low as 20 percent and as high as 60 percent. At some point between 20 percent and 60 percent of Negro occupancy, white dwellers will abandon the housing, leaving it to become entirely Negro. The argument is that if integrated housing is to be maintained, housing officials must adopt policies regulating Negro occupancy well within permissible tipping-point limitations and thus avoid the flight of whites. It should be noted that housing and social science experts are no longer in as complete agreement as they once were about the necessity and advantages of controlled Negro occupancy in integrated housing situations. The concept still has many ardent adherents.

The legal difficulty with this theory is that the concept of the individual's right to equal treatment and freedom from racial discrimination is firmly implanted in American constitutional doctrine, and the showing of group interest would appear to be no answer to the right claimed by the individual. Indeed, if group interest had been considered paramount, many of the decisions by our courts outlawing discrimination might never have been written.

In the early days of court litigation attacking instances of segregation and discrimination, the defense always sought to interpose the argument that the segregated school had been erected at the request of Negroes, or that there was no general need in the Negro community for the course of study being demanded, or that the segregated union local had been created at the insistence of Negro workers. The courts gave short shrift to these contentions, relying on the theory that the individual was entitled to vindicate his constitutional claim and could not be thwarted by the action or the passivity of other persons.

Proponents of the benign-quota thesis argue that courts should depart in this instance from the usual formula and sustain benign quotas against attack, on the grounds that, on balance, the social good achieved through the use of quotas, in stabilizing and in helping to spread pockets of integrated housing, more than compensates for whatever individual hurt might be inflicted. The colored applicant, refused because he exceeds the quota allocated to Negroes, although he may feel individual chagrin, cannot complain, since his group was accorded equality of treatment. Thus far no attempt to apply quotas in the public housing field has been upheld by courts that have had occasion to examine them.

The practical difficulty with the quota concept is that quotas are not benign and never can be in any true sense. They are discriminatory; the people upon whom they are imposed are treated differently from the rest of the general public. What the advocates of benign quotas are saying in the final analysis is that prejudice against Negroes will be with us for many years to come; that Negroes must accept unequal treatment; that if the imposition of quotas in a variety of housing situations succeeds in giving significant impetus to integrated housing, we will be on the road to a completely open housing market. In short, quotas are only a temporary expedient to give integration a chance to get off the ground. Unfortunately, what may well be accomplished is merely a somewhat less prohibitive restriction on the Negro's entry into the general housing market, and symbolic or token residential integration.

Negroes themselves can only be ambivalent at best about benign quotas. They have to personally resent the fact that neither they nor members of their race are able to buy a home or rent an apartment on the same terms as other people. Not only must a Negro meet whatever requirements are generally imposed, but if he is over the number allotted to his group, his application will be rejected. And when he is accepted, he must face mentally and emotionally this same situation again and again as other Negro applicants are turned down. I remember becoming furious on accidentally learning that in a housing unit in which Negro occupancy was controlled in the interest of integrated living, accommodations to a Negro friend of mine, with an application of long standing, had been refused, while several of my white friends, who had just sought entry, were being offered apartments. I could intellectualize about the larger wisdom of the restriction to guard against white exodus, but the actual situation posed too great a threat through my two sets of friends to my own sense of worth and self-esteem. My mental process, therefore, could not prevent a feeling of outrage and indignation at the injustices my Negro friend suffered because of his color.

II

My real objection to discussion of these concepts in the context of American race relations is that one is engaged in an interesting but abstract intellectual exercise. What reason is there to debate the legality or wisdom of preferential treatment, when we are not even close to winning the war against discrimination? It is true, of course, that pundits forecast that even if discrimination were to be completely eliminated tomorrow, something more would be required for Negroes to achieve equality in any real sense. This certainly would appear to be grounded in realism, and yet it is impossible for us now to envision what would happen in a society with all racial barriers removed. What we must concentrate on is the elimination of discrimination—only then may discussion about preferences become pertinent to the question of equal treatment.

More dangerously, debate about the wisdom of compensation, preferences, and even benign quotas, insofar as Negroes are concerned, distorts and obscures the basic problem that our society now faces and must resolve. Ours is a racist social order; despite our supposed dedication to the principle of equality without reference to race, color, or previous condition, the white skin is regarded as inherently superior and the black skin as innately inferior.

The scientific consensus that race or color differences do not predetermine individual capabilities is accepted as a theoretical proposition, but our lives are regulated and ordered by rules that accord the white skin a superior place. And this is our fundamental sickness. We know that we are supposed to believe that all men are equal, but we do not; and we have to justify somewhat our lack or failure to live up to what we know is right and just.

To serve that need, we have created a great American myth—the myth of steady progress in race relations and of a history of constant improvement in the Negro's status. Every significant event that can be interpreted as a step toward equal opportunity and equal justice is celebrated as if the final objective had been realized. The United States Supreme Court decision outlawing segregation in education was treated for a time as if it had at last settled the race problem. Americans do not want to face the reality of the Negro's position in our society; thus, Negroes and whites join in perpetuating a race relations legend.

Today, newspapers are concentrating on what is called the "white backlash" in reaction to the "Negro revolution." In short, the inference from use of this terminology is that Negro progress has been so phenomenal that white people are beginning to react against it. The real facts are that the so-called Negro revolution is merely a drastic break with the traditional Negro image. No great improvements in the Negro's status have as yet been accomplished. Although white America is beginning to take

a closer look at the race problem, it merely glances fear-
fully and fitfully. This is a healthy departure, I suppose,
since the country has refused to recognize the real dimen-
sion of the problem for almost seventy-five years. The
revolution is a change in stance and temperament. The
patient, happy, contented Negro has been replaced by
one who is impatient, discontented, and who is demanding his rights now. As the Negro's protest has grown more
militant, with resort to direct action, whites, who previously had no need to manifest their prejudices in public,
have begun to do so. Since Negroes have become bolder
in demanding the removal of all vestiges of slavery, which
have kept them shackled in subjugation, whites have become bolder in insisting that the fetters not be removed.
All that has happened is that Negroes and whites are
being more open and candid in revealing their true senti-
ments.

I put the discussion of quota, preference, and compensatory treatment in the same myth-maintaining category. If we debate about these questions, we can pretend
that the problem of discrimination itself has been solved.
We have progressed so far along the road toward our
goal that we can cross the next bridge—what next, now
that equality has been provided? Negroes allowed themselves to be drawn into this debate in the summer of 1964
in reference to contentions about according Negroes job
preferences. What Negroes were really talking about and
are presently seeking is a real-life manifestation that employment discrimination is no longer practiced. This

means more than a token force of Negroes in particular institutions. It means that employers must hire a substantial number of colored employees. To me this is not the same as arguing for preferential hiring. It is merely asking for effective implementation of a policy of nondiscrimination.

No institution in this country is free of racial bias, and this includes the Federal Government and New York City as employers—two establishments that can now point to the best records on the nondiscrimination evaluator. There has been no substantial change in the Negro's position vis-à-vis white America in one hundred years of freedom. He has made gains, of course; his lot has improved when measured against his past, but his relative position compared with the gains of other groups has remained relatively constant—one of disadvantage, depression, and abject inequality. Negroes have not been accorded equal treatment, even in those cases where their qualifications cannot be questioned. The fact that Negroes are not being employed is principally the result of discrimination, and is not usually caused by an inability to find qualified Negroes to fill certain jobs. In some instances, employers do seek certain skills and are unable to find Negroes who possess them, but in most cases discrimination is the reason Negroes are absent from the work force.

There has been a slow erosion of some of the most burdensome racial barriers, but this has not come through a steady and progressive lowering of hurdles. In terms of gains achieved, the Negro's struggle toward equality is one of fits and starts—two steps forward and one back, a long pause, and then two steps forward and one back. It is more akin to the ebb and flow of the tide, and in this connection the Goldwater candidacy and the California housing referendum are cause for grave concern about the future among all civil rights advocates.

Rigid segregation, which has been described as a way of life by Southern whites—indigenous to and a commonplace of Southern living since time immemorial, we have been led to believe—is of relatively recent vintage, a twentieth-century phenomenon. A strict pattern of racial segregation and discrimination became a fixture of Washington, D. C., with the Wilson administration, and Negroes were barred from jobs and segregated in public facilities heretofore open to them. More recently, the Federal public housing programs and urban renewal programs and procedures have helped entrench housing segregation in the North, making that problem and its progeny, de facto school segregation, seem all but insoluble.

Widespread discrimination against Negroes exists today in all aspects of American life and in all areas of the United States. Before Northern-style discrimination was carefully examined, it was assumed that the race problem would be resolved once discrimination was no longer formalized and mandated into laws requiring segregation in schools, in transportation, in places of public accommodations, and in employment, and once the Negro was no longer disenfranchised throughout the South. The civil rights organizations at one time focused almost all of their efforts and energies on the open racist policies of the Southern states. The legal foundation for these raw forms of discriminatory practices in the South was shorn away by the United States Supreme Court's decision in 1954 outlawing segregation in the nation's public schools. Thereafter, it soon became evident that more than effective implementation of that decision throughout the South would be necessary, if Negroes were going to cross over the River Jordan to freedom's land. For in the North, which had repealed most of its segregation laws early in the twentieth century and had begun to enact antidiscrimination and civil rights laws of various kinds, Negroes were kept separate and apart from whites and were still confined to particular residential areas, to certain of the public schools, and were barred from various kinds of employment.

Discrimination against Negroes was and is a part of the fabric of American life in New York, Chicago, and San Francisco, as well as in Jackson, Mississippi; Little Rock, Arkansas; and Birmingham, Alabama. It inheres in the housing market and the services of real estate brokers, landlords, builders, developers (private and public), city planners, banks, and mortgage loan companies. Up to now, despite the existence of fair housing laws in 19 states and ordinances in 49 municipalities and an executive order requiring the elimination of discrimination in respect to housing affected by Federal programs, local housing officials, particularly those administering the public housing programs, have been left free to segregate according to neighborhood patterns and occupancy and have been restricted only by the requirement to provide equitably for the families of all races determined by the volume and urgency of their respective needs. Past practices have virtually solidified housing segregation in the North, and as yet no major break in the iron ring enclosing the Negro ghetto has been effected.

Discrimination is engrained in public school systems to the extent that Negro children are attending schools that are segregated in fact and which are concededly providing them with inadequate and inferior education. It includes public employment opportunities at the Federal, state, and local levels; employment resulting from services performed by private industry for governmental agencies pursuant to contract; employment opportunities resulting from public grants made for specific scientific, industrial, and educational projects; and employment that is purely private. It includes vocational rehabilitation and retraining, and educational and training opportunities which are sponsored, encouraged, stimulated, or supplied by the government and directly or indirectly financed by public funds. It embraces job recruitment and referrals, by both public and private agencies, and on-the-job training and upgrading. Government, management, and labor unions bear a direct responsibility for the perpetuation of discrimination by virtue of practices and procedures approved, endorsed, and maintained by them.

Let me suggest that we must concern ourselves with

finding a workable and effective methodology for ending discrimination before quotas, preferences, or compensation can become even relevant or a troublesome problem meriting debate.

III

The entire Negro community today is in the throes of a devastating economic crisis, with a rate of unemployment double or triple that of whites. The United States Department of Labor in 1964 estimated the Negro unemployment rate at 12.2 percent; the national rate is 6.4 percent. Negroes constitute 24 percent of the long-term unemployed.

Contrary to the popular notion, the last two decades have not been periods of uninterrupted progress and expanding economic opportunity for the Negro. Indeed, the income gap between Negroes and whites, which lessened during World War II, has remained virtually stable ever since. In 1947 the median wage of the Negro was 54 percent of that of whites; in 1962 it was 55 percent. In fact, there has been a widening of the gap in actual income, so that today the dollar differential between Negroes and whites is spreading. The median income for Negroes is $3191 as compared to $5981 for whites. While the proportion of Negro families in the $4000–6000 income bracket has tripled in the last twenty years, 60 percent of the Negro families today earn less than $4000 as compared to 28 percent of the whites; and 75 percent of all Negro families have income lower than the median $5981 income of whites.

Nor has there been any relative change in the Negro's occupational status in the past twenty years. Whatever rise in his occupational level can be demonstrated is chiefly the result of his migration from the rural South to urban industrial areas, from the farm to the mining and manufacturing industries where unskilled and semiskilled labor were in plentiful demand, rather than any major improvement in job opportunities. Negro migration from the rural South to urban industrial areas has grown in such proportions that the 1960 census figures revealed close to 50 percent of the Negro population is now settled outside the South. Moreover, Negro populations of New York, Chicago, Philadelphia, Detroit, and Los Angeles exceed that of any city in the South. Unfortunately, the Negro migration to the Northern cities has come at a time when job opportunities for the unskilled and poorly educated have begun to shrink.

Between 1940 and 1960 there was a net increase of 19,000,000 jobs, but a decrease of 4,600,000 jobs in agriculture, mining, and production. The increase has occurred chiefly in the white-collar categories, which have been traditionally difficult of entry for Negroes. In 1962 only 17 percent of Negroes, in contrast to 47 percent of whites, were white-collar employees. Even in the blue-collar field the ratio of Negro to white job holders fell between 1955 and 1962 to levels prevailing in 1948.

The Negro's lack of education hurts, but does not tell

the whole story. There are one million Negro illiterates out of a total of three million in that category. Twenty-five percent of the Negro adult population (2.3 million) did not complete five years of schooling, in contrast to only 7 percent of whites with this disability. Fifty percent of the Negro adult population did not finish elementary school, as compared to 25 percent of the white adult population.

Negroes, as is to be expected, are concentrated in the low-paid occupations as laborers or service workers, and eight of ten Negroes with an eighth-grade education work in unskilled jobs, but only three of ten whites of the same educational level are confined to unskilled labor. And, paradoxically, the earning gap between Negroes and whites increases with educational attainment. The Negro doctor's earning capacity and lifetime earning expectations are roughly half those of the white doctor. The average Negro college graduate's lifetime earnings are less than that of the average white person who has only completed grade school. Thus, it is clear that underemployment of Negroes is another facet of the problem of discrimination to which he is subjected.

Negroes now form a large percentage of the hard core of the permanently unemployed—the unemployables. The bread and butter of their sustenance comes now, as in the past, from unskilled and semiskilled labor. Unfortunately, these are the jobs most severely affected by retrenchment caused by economic layoffs and modernization resulting from technological changes. Thus, to the

Negro worker a slight recession may result in economic ruin. And unemployment promises to continue at an even more accelerated pace as technological advances make increasingly obsolete and unneeded semiskilled and unskilled labor, which the Negro traditionally performs.

Where outright unemployment is not a problem, instability of employment persists. Since 1958, many Negroes have been spending several weeks to months annually in idleness, in search of another job after a previous one folded.

The foregoing figures are only part of the story. Discrimination, poverty, and unemployment go hand in hand, reaping their social and psychological produce—lack of hope, feelings of futility and helplessness, greater and greater alienation, social hostility, and worse. This growing despair, loss of hope, and sense of helplessness is evidenced by the fact that in 1952, of males between twenty-five and sixty-four years of age, 5.4 percent of nonwhites and 4.5 percent of whites were not seeking employment. In 1963 the percentages were 8.2 percent of nonwhites and 4.9 percent of whites—growing evidence that the Negro feels he is fighting against a stone wall.

Discrimination in employment is a universal pattern, and even the government discriminates as an employer. While improvement can be shown in Federal employment since 1961, here as elsewhere Negroes are clustered in the lower-paying jobs and woefully absent from the higher administrative and professional levels. Vast sums of public monies are spent in national defense and on public construction and in other services performed by private industry. The Federal Government and some state and municipal agencies require all persons or firms under contract to sign a nondiscrimination pledge. Even without such contract provisions, the Constitution would appear to bar discrimination by those who contract to perform publicly financed services. Yet, despite some progress by the President's Committee on Equal Employment Opportunities and the existence of approximately 23 state Fair Employment Practices laws and 35 municipal ordinances, there is little distinction between the pattern of discrimination in those industries with and those without government contracts. And in respect to public construction where craft unions control hiring, recruitment, and selection for apprentice training, Negroes are all but completely excluded.

Federal, state, and local funds in the amount of $228,000,000 are spent on vocational training annually; 3,750,000 students and 90,000 teachers are involved in these programs. The primary purpose of this training is to teach a basic trade and industrial skill and to provide training for occupations in science and technology of importance to national defense. Governmental regulations ensure discrimination and public funds support and encourage discrimination by providing for training in jobs traditionally open to the applicant's group. For Negroes, training under these programs is too often limited to the menial and lowest jobs (for which there is less and less future need), whereas whites are taught newer skills, ensuring them steady future employment. In the main, for example, whites are trained in industrial electronics, mechanical drafting, plumbing, tool and die design, electronics, aircraft, and general sheet metal work. Negroes receive training in short-order cooking, dry cleaning, tailoring, and designing.

Another example is the Federal Manpower Development and Training Program, which seeks to retrain unemployed persons to suit them for new jobs. Obviously, because Negro workers are extremely vulnerable to unemployment, they more than any other group qualify for admission to this program. Again, reports indicate that Negroes are being limited to programs that simply perpetuate their traditional concentration in menial and unskilled jobs. In some places, it was learned, there were all-Negro programs for chambermaids and waitresses; in others, all-white programs for electronic machine operators, with Negroes being restricted to laundry machine and shirt pressers training. Because of the statutory requirements that there shall be a reasonable expectation of employment as the basis for admission to training, Negroes are being screened out of acceptance for training in skilled crafts even in Northern areas.

The Bureau of Apprenticeship and Training of the United States Department of Labor has responsibility for stimulating apprentice training activity and providing technical assistance to apprentice groups. The Federal Government does not give any money for direct support of these programs, but programs must meet Bureau standards to be registered. Registration provides the legal basis for various direct and indirect public subsidies. Classroom instruction is an integral part of all registered programs, and vocational training programs and grants-in-aid often provide the classrooms and pay for teachers. Admission to training in most cases is governed by a joint union-employer committee. About 60 percent of these programs are for training in the construction crafts, the bulk of the nonconstruction training being in printing, skilled machine, and metal trades.

Until 1961, the Bureau made no attempt to remedy the almost total denial to Negroes of opportunities for participation in apprentice training. Nondiscrimination clauses are now included in all new apprenticeship training agreements with all firms under contract to the Federal Government. In addition, in June 1963 the Secretary of Labor announced the formulation of standards of objectivity, designed to secure selection of a number of qualified applicants who would otherwise be improperly discriminated against, to encourage steps in regard to application lists to offset previous discriminatory practices, and to encourage nondiscrimination in all phases of apprenticeship and employment during apprenticeship operation selection. While these are good beginnings, they will have only limited effect unless and until training is geared to the nation's need for skilled workers, rather than the union's limited goal of ensuring full employment for its members, and the selection process and training must be in the control of public agencies.

The United States spends millions of dollars in Federal grants for the operation of the United States Employment Service, whose principal function is finding jobs for the unemployed and finding workers for the employer. These agencies receive funds and rewards based in great part on the number of gross placements made during the year. Thus, operating personnel are encouraged to fill discriminatory job orders, to make selections on the basis of race because the applicant is more likely to be hired, and to persist in patterns of colored and white jobs. Thus, again, discrimination is fostered.

Labor unions are directly responsible for a great deal of the discrimination that is presently a part of the labor market. Labor union discrimination of concern to us takes several forms—outright union exclusion, particularly prevalent in the building construction, crafts, and skilled metal trade unions; and exclusion from the apprenticeship training programs. The latter form of discrimination deprives Negroes of the opportunity to obtain training essential to master the craft. It takes place because of union control over selection of persons who enter upon apprentice training. And outright discrimination is deadly in the construction industry and metal trades. These are areas of great activity, but Negroes are particularly frozen out of all skilled jobs.

Management is generally indifferent, if not outright discriminatory. In areas where antidiscrimination laws are in effect, the result has been that management has opened up to Negroes some jobs heretofore closed. But Negroes are not usually considered for positions that lead to high administrative or managerial posts within the firm, plant, or industry. Where skilled crafts or trades are involved, the union barrier has proved all but insurmountable, since normally management has been content to acquiesce in the union-imposed discrimination or has used it as a rationalization for its own discriminatory policies.

In the supervision of Federal programs designed to train for or secure jobs, the government must abandon practices and procedures that tend to perpetuate discrimination. The practice, for example, of allocation of funds for the United States Employment Service based upon the gross number of job referrals for the previous year is an inducement to countenance discrimination, as is the requirement that vocational training be given for available job opportunities.

The Federal Government must strictly enforce the antidiscrimination provisions in its contracts with private agencies. That responsibility does not cease with the signing of the contract. The government must supervise and implement enforcement of an antidiscrimination policy in regard to recruitment, employment, on-the-job training, and upgrading.

The government's apprentice training program must be geared to the training of a sufficient supply of skilled labor to meet the country's future needs. This means that the government will have to take responsibility for opening up apprentice training to all without discrimination based upon color—not, as now, merely promulgating regulations to that effect without implementing them. Until the government takes over the task of selecting, screening, training, and certifying of apprentices, discrimination in this area will not be cured.

Approximately 23 states have statutes barring discrimination in employment, and the 1964 Federal Civil Rights Act has a fair unemployment practices provision scheduled to become operative in part in July 1965. One of the serious weaknesses in the operation of many municipal and state fair employment commissions is that they are limited to functioning as complaint-taking agencies. Unless these agencies are empowered to concentrate their efforts on securing compliance with the state or municipal law, little headway against discrimination will be made. At present, the burden falls too heavily on the Negro complainant, who must know the law, know the steps to take to invoke it, and be sufficiently motivated to move. He must apply for a job at places where he knows, or believes from past experience or out of general knowledge, that application is fruitless and will be refused. He must know that refusal on basis of race is illegal and that there is a state or city agency to which he can go for help. He must locate that agency, and take time off to go there to be interviewed by a member of its staff. If the Commission believes his case has possibilities, then he is required to spend many future hours and days conferring with them, through the process of complaint drawing, adjustment, conciliation, and possibly hearings.

Only the most sophisticated person can manage all this. For antidiscrimination laws to be really effective, the government must assume through these agencies a more aggressive and affirmative role in the fight against employment discrimination. The Commissions must be empowered to investigate and initiate proceedings against employers and labor unions without a complaint. The absence or token presence of Negroes in various businesses, concerns, in apprentice and on-the-job training, should constitute a *prima facie* case of discrimination, which can be rebutted by a showing that Negroes are not present because of factors having no relation to discrimination. Moreover, where a pattern of discrimination is revealed, the Commission should be empowered to require the establishment of policies and procedures of recruitment, employment, on-the-job training, and upgrading and apprenticeship to remedy the discrimination —not merely to order the employment of the particular complainant.

The Negro's high visibility has been a deterrent to the easing of his disadvantaged status and his disappearance in America's melting pot. It should be helpful in any full-fledged effort to implement a policy of nondiscrimination in employment. On-the-spot inspection will reveal whether Negroes are present in the work force, and roughly in what capacities. Formal pledges between private contractors and government to enforce a nondiscrimination clause which then remains unenforced is meaningless. Laws that announce a policy of equal treatment, but which are not fully effectuated mislead the public into believing that more progress has been made than the true evidence would warrant.

Some of these procedures are now being followed by the President's Committee on Equal Employment Opportunities, but the state Commissions are, in general, only able to initiate informal complaints, and in such cases, they cannot issue corrective orders that are enforceable in the courts. These laws should be amended to permit the agencies to initiate complaints, and empower them to issue cease and desist orders, enforceable in courts. Despite this limitation, the initiative process ought to be more widely used, and it should encompass industry-wide patterns. Publication alone of discriminatory practices that exist should help. Large corporations, guilty of such misconduct, would not want it to be a matter of wide public notice.

Both the Federal and state governments—wherever public funds are made available for training—must seek to carry out a program of education and encouragement, to involve Negroes in learning skilled trades and crafts.

Management has the responsibility of promulgating and enforcing an active and aggressive program of recruiting Negro employees and of encouraging Negroes to obtain the necessary skills for work in their plants or institutions. They ought to seek out promising Negro youths for on-the-job training; and they should make it clear that qualified Negroes, now barred by barriers of race or color, will be welcome in their plants. This is not preferential hiring or discrimination in reverse. It is merely recognition of the reality that without active encouragement and recruitment, the picture in respect to Negro employment will not change. Industry must also not acquiesce in any discrimination practiced by unions. Its policy of nondiscrimination must be firm and aggressive, and it must make periodic investigations of its own plant and personnel practices to make certain that these policies are being carried out. This does not mean that management needs to enforce a policy of personnel record-keeping with racial identifications. On-the-site investigations by management will usually suffice to determine whether its policy is being implemented in the various departments and divisions under its control. A negative policy of nondiscrimination does not suffice. Unless nondiscrimination is aggressively endorsed and vigorously implemented, unless all subordinates involved in execution of the policy are made aware that this constitutes a firm and irrevocable decision, the policy will be only fitfully effective.

What should concern us and occupy our attention are changes in recruitment and employment practices. Irving Ferman, at one time Executive Vice Chairman of the President's Committee on Government Contracts, writing for the New York Law University Law Forum in 1960, has stated the matter well:

The fact is that job discrimination on grounds of color, race, creed or national origin is not normally an isolated event. It is a type of group behavior, for although one individual in a position of power may be responsible for the discriminatory acts or actions per se, he will always be found to have the tacit support or at the very best the permissive indifference of his fellow members of management and even of some community leaders in the area in which the concern is situated.

The job of integrating minority group members, particularly Negroes, into the work force, actually gets done only when [management assumes] the affirmative duty to make specific commitments. These are specific only when they spell out the fact that a definite number of qualified Negroes will be employed within a given period of time in jobs from which they have been traditionally barred.

Directing contractors to put up posters publicly setting forth their obligations under the nondiscrimination clause, helping to formulate nondiscriminatory personnel policies which stipulate that applications from all qualified persons will be accepted, and hoping that some day a qualified Negro will apply and be hired, does not break the ice in this job integration process.

There is need for more full-time school counselors, particularly in schools with appreciable numbers of non-white children. There is need for more clinical and psychiatric services in schools to counteract the spirit-deadening pressures of the environment. There must be extensive use of guidance counselors whose responsibility and basic function is to uncover and encourage nonwhite talented youth. In addition to guidance for youth, Negro parents and neighborhood groups also must be helped with guidance and counseling, so that their own feeling of despair and frustration will not unduly impede and hinder their children from breaking the shackles of caste and color discrimination and investing in the future by learning skills and trades not heretofore open to Negroes. Employment agency personnel, both public and private, should make an effort to become skilled in the finding and placement of specialized minority group personnel.

Under our system, while individual liberty is a precious right, that liberty can be curbed and restricted for the greater common good. Moreover, the right to engage in a lawful calling is a basic right of every American. Hence, the power of Federal or state government to bar racial discrimination in employment is no longer open to question. Nor is there doubt that discrimination cannot be practiced by governmental authority, either directly or indirectly. Thus, any publicly sponsored program or one supported by public funds is subject to the constitutional proscriptions barring racial or color differentiations. All government practices that foster and perpetuate discrimination, therefore, would appear to be illegal under present constitutional doctrine. The problem in attempting to pose this issue in court litigation is a procedural one: who has standing to sue? Moreover, under a recent ruling of the National Labor Relations Board in *Hughes Tool*, the National Labor Relations Act makes any union-imposed or -induced discrimination against Negro workers in the terms and conditions of employment or in their status in the union an unfair labor practice.

Finally, more adequate enforcement of present law,

and recognition by public agencies of their legal responsibility not to practice or foster discrimination, would help in alleviating the present situation. The new Federal Civil Rights Act, depending upon the manner of its administration, could become a most effective weapon to ensure equal employment for Negroes.

The task would be eased, of course, with full employment. White fears and opposition would abate somewhat. But the history of employment in the last twenty years makes clear beyond doubt that discrimination against Negroes is only incidentally the result of a tightening of general employment opportunities or the absence of qualified Negroes to fill various jobs. The country has accepted employment discrimination as a pattern of life. It has demanded that Negroes accept this as what should be. It has refused to face that fact that what has been demanded and acted upon by all American institutions is acquiescence in the application and implementation of a racist policy to the Negro's detriment. We must deal with that wrong and take steps to eliminate that policy, before we need concern ourselves with the intriguing implications of preferential hiring.

Subsequent to *Brown* v. *Board of Education* in 1954, the United States Supreme Court began to use "racial segregation" and "discrimination" interchangeably. That decision marks a divide in American life. Yet, as fundamental a break with the past as *Brown* was, it too was formulated on the concept that the Negro must willingly bear the burden of discrimination for a time and forego immediate vindication of that to which he is entitled under the Constitution. This was the basis of the Court-allowed postponement of desegregation of the public schools under an "all deliberate speed" timetable.

If we look at the statistics, the picture is bleak. Late in 1964, only about 2 percent of the Negro children in the eleven states of the Old Confederacy were actually in classrooms with white children.

Most school districts in the South have taken the Supreme Court's "with all deliberate speed" to mean an agonizing, slowed-up transformation—no move until a lawsuit, and then, when forced by court order, to desegregate a grade a year, starting either at grade 1 and moving upward or at grade 12 moving downward, and with as few Negroes involved as possible.

In Alabama, 11 Negroes out of a total Negro school population of 287,414 are going to schools with white children. In Arkansas, of 112,012 total Negro public school enrollment, 1084 are going to school with whites. In Florida, of some 237,871 Negro students enrolled in the public schools, 3650 are actually attending schools with whites. Of 337,534 Negro students enrolled in the public schools in Georgia, 177 are attending schools with white children. Of 301,433 Negro students enrolled in Louisiana, 1814 are attending school with whites. Of 346,746 Negro students enrolled in public schools in North Carolina, 1865 are attending schools with whites. Of the 258,955 Negroes in public schools in South Carolina, 10 are attending schools with white children. Of the

164,940 Negro students attending schools in Tennessee, 4466 are actually in classrooms with whites. Of 326,409 Negro students in attendance in schools in Texas, 14,000 are actually in classrooms with whites. Of the 236,386 Negro students in the public schools in Virginia, 3721 are actually in classrooms with whites. In Mississippi, a few Negro school children are just now beginning to attend classes with white children. In the border states, the figure is much better. In the public schools in Delaware 55.4 percent of the Negroes are actually in classrooms with white children; 54.1 percent is the figure in Kentucky; 48.3 percent in Maryland; 42.1 percent in Missouri; 28.1 percent in Oklahoma; 87.9 percent in West Virginia.

The *Brown* decision was historic, not because of what it has accomplished in the field of education, but because of the transformation it has made in the whole complex of race relations in this country. *Brown* foretold that all government-imposed racial segregation was unconstitutional; that all publicly enforced, sponsored, or supported racial discrimination was beyond the pale; that equal rights legislation in the North was not a bounty, the gracious gift of a more liberal-minded and enlightened citizenry. It was mandated by the fundamental law—the birthright of every American.

The Negro was no longer a suppliant, seeking, begging, pleading to be invested with full citizenship. Equal treatment was his to demand, to insist upon, and where this was denied to him, he was being robbed of his constitutional heritage. This new legal position of the Negro propelled him into an insistent militancy.

He soon saw that outside the South Negroes attended public schools that were largely Negro, particularly at the elementary school level. Public school officials in the urban North had effectuated a separation of Negro and whites in the public schools that generally followed the color line that separated Negro and white residential areas. Moreover, it was clear that these schools were not performing the function of providing Negro children with the necessary educational tools to enable them to compete for better jobs and occupations, thereby improving their status in our society.

In general, the Negro schools in the urban North are academically behind the other public schools; they are overcrowded; they are headed by principals and administrators who, until recently, rationalized the poor academic standings of their schools on the theory that the child could not be expected to do any better. School failures have been attributed to outside factors—the home, poverty, lack of education of the parents. Certainly, the circumstances under which the school was expected to impart learning were unusually demoralizing. The children were from crowded slum areas; their experiences were totally at war with those of the middle-class teachers who were charged with motivating them to learn basic academic skills and with arousing in them an avid curiosity for learning. This was at best a formidable task, and for a time school authorities retreated behind the general folklore—the basic incapacities of Negroes, their disinterest, and their inability to amass knowledge on the same terms as the white child.

One of the results of the recent complaints of Negroes about the inadequacies of educational offerings afforded their children is that educators who yesterday were placing academic failure on Negro parents, home environment, and the lack of intellectual stimulation are now beginning to experiment with teaching methodology specifically geared to the background and experiences of the underprivileged Negro child. Although all the results are not in, it seems evident that this is the direction in which educational authorities must move in an honest attempt to improve the quality of education offered underprivileged nonwhite children.

It is in connection with education that we hear most proposals for compensatory treatment. The quality of education in the public schools must be improved, and the school must be prepared to meet the specific needs of the child from the slums, the migrant from the rural South, the produce of families that have lost all hope. But compensation cannot be the answer to desegregation. Negro children cannot secure equal educational opportunities in schools that are in fact segregated and isolated from the main educational current of the community in which they live. The truth is that schools that are in fact segregated are regarded as inferior, low-status schools in the eyes of the community. No matter how well a school so regarded may measure up in respect to plant and physical facilities,

against schools not so stigmatized, the intangibles are decisive because in the final analysis the school atmosphere
is determinative. Those who have a choice would not send
their children to these low-status schools.

The United States Supreme Court recognized the importance of these intangibles in deciding whether equality
of education is being provided in the constitutional sense.
In 1950, in a case involving a Negro student in the graduate school at the University of Oklahoma, the Court
found that although McLaurin had the same teachers, the
same books, and was taught in the same classroom, the
fact that he was subjected to rules not applicable to
the general public by being required to sit in a special seat
in the class and at a special table in the library made it
impossible for him to obtain that equality of educational
offering the law required. And in a case involving determination of whether a segregated law school was the
equal of the University of Texas, the Court placed stress
on the attitude of the community.

The present controversy in New York about the school
board's attempt to make a start toward integration is not
over bussing or the neighborhood school, but is based on
fear that school reorganization that brings Negro and
white children in school together will have a harmful educational effect on the white child. The controversy is an
unquestioned admission by the white parents involved
(Parents and Taxpayers Association) that they believe the
Negro school to be inferior. Proposals for compensatory
treatment under these circumstances is a dishonest ration-

alization. It is unlikely that the white community, which has heretofore neglected quality in Negro schools, will ever in fact agree to underwrite the costs involved in an intensified "higher horizons" program in schools in the Negro area. During the late 1940s and early 1950s, when the drive against enforced segregation in schools in the South had begun, the white South, which up to that point had placed great emphasis on the "separate" but little on the "equal" aspects of the "separate but equal" equation by which segregation was justified, began to make feverish attempts to improve the quality of Negro schools. The Negro child cannot obtain equality of education confined to his ghetto—he must become a part of this culture, and he can do so only by having the opportunity of being taught in a school situation along with other people. Desegregation and quality education must be given equal stress.

IV

The Negro is in a precarious status in the United States. He has not been accorded the opportunity to enjoy the fruits of full citizenship. For many years, to most of us, this was merely standard operating procedure—regrettable, perhaps, but a situation that Negroes had to accept. Until recently, it was expected that their patience in acceptance of permanent subordination in our society would continue for years to come. But in 1954, the United States Supreme Court held in effect that under our basic law the Negro was entitled to live in this country without the onus of state-enforced restrictions and delimitations based on color. The legal basis for the Negro's subservience was swept away.

That decision has brought about a revolutionary change in the Negro's stance vis-à-vis white America. He is insisting on having what the Constitution says is rightfully his, and having it now. The Negro's actual inferiority in our society is based on more than a legally fixed status; he has been confined to the lowest and meanest position in our society by custom and usage, by the fact that our social order is actually, although not in principle, ruled on the postulate of white supremacy. Discrimination is rampant against Negroes in housing, in schools, in employment—indeed, in all aspects of American life. Many thoughtful Americans are now convinced that we cannot keep our promise of equal treatment without taking special measures, other than the mere elimination of discrimination. For this reason the issue of benign quotas in housing, preferential hiring, and compensatory education are being debated as appropriate tools to help make equal treatment a reality. While benign quotas give me pause, I do not object to these proposals on moral or legal grounds. The proposal for preferential employment for Negroes will undoubtedly be overwhelmingly opposed by the average white person. But I take issue with these propositions because they are unrealistic in the face of the present status of race relations. The suggestion that the time has come for us to consider imposing benign quotas, preferences, or compensatory treatment fosters the fallacy that discrimination has been eliminated. Since that task is far from finished, I would suggest that our energy and intellect be expended on promulgating and implementing methods for accomplishing that goal, before concerning ourselves with these steps we may have to take once a shield of effective nondiscrimination has been forged.

Some Source Materials Where Facets of the Problem Are Discussed

On Employment

Testimony of Undersecretary of Labor John F. Hennings, before United States Senate Committee on Labor and Public Works, Hearings on Equal Employment Opportunity, 88th Cong., 1st Sess. (1963)

Testimony of Dr. Herman Miller, Asst. to Director of United States Census Bureau, *idem*

Vivian W. Henderson, *The Economic Status of Negroes,* Southern Regional Council (1963)

United States Department of Labor, Report on Manpower Requirements, Resources, Utilization and Training (1963)

United States Department of Labor, Report on Manpower Requirements, Resources, Utilization and Training (1964)

Matthew A. Kessler, "Economic Status of Non-White

Workers," United States Department of Labor, Bureau of Labor Statistics, Special Labor Force, Report No. 33, 8 (1963), Reprint July 1963 *Monthly Labor Review*

United States Bureau of Census, *Current Population Reports*, ser. P-60, No. 41 (1963)

Field, "A New Look at Employment," 42 *N.C.L. Rev.* 154 (1963)

Employment, United States Commission on Civil Rights Report No. 3 (1961)

For Housing Data

Home Finance Agency, "State Statistics and Local Ordinances and Resolutions Prohibiting Discrimination in Housing and Urban Renewal Operations," No. 21 (1961)

For Benign Quota Debate

Note, "Benign Quotas: A Plea For Integrated Private Housing," 70 *Yale L.J.* 126 (1961)

Charles Abrams, *Forbidden Neighbors,* 312 (N.Y., Harper 1955)

Peter Marcuse, "Benign Quotas Re-examined," 3 *J. Intergroup Rel.* 102 (1962)

Robert Weaver, "Integration in Public Housing," *Annals* 86 (1956)

The school desegregation figures are from a statistical survey published by the Southern Educational Service in April 1964. Since in September 1964 a new school term began, these figures are not exact. However, no appreciable revision in these figures will be necessitated.

General

Preferential Hiring for Negroes: A Debate, 45 *American Child*, No. 4 (1963)

Civil Rights, Report of United States Commission on Civil Rights (1963)

Paul H. Norgen and Samuel E. Hill, *Toward Fair Employment* (N.Y., Columbia U. Press 1964)

Irving Ferman, "Discrimination in Employment," 6 *N.Y. University Law Forum*, 60 (1960)

C. Vann Woodward, *The Strange Career of Jim Crow* (N.Y., Oxford University Press 1955)

Cases Where Some Facet of Problem Is Discussed

Missouri ex rel Gaines v. Canada, 305 U.S. 337 (1938)

Sipuel v. Board of Regents, 332 U.S. 631 (1948)

Brown v. Board of Education, 347 U.S. 483 (1954)

McLaurin v. Board of Regents, 337 U.S. 637 (1950)

Sweatt v. Painter, 337 U.S. 629 (1950)

Banks v. California Housing Authority, 120 Cal. App. 2d 1, 260 P2d 668 (1953), certiorari denied, 347 U.S. 974 (1954)

Taylor v. Leonard, 30 N.J. Sup. 116, 103 A2d 632 (1954)

Independent Metal Workers Union, Local No. 1 (Hughes Tool Co.), 147 NLRB, No. 166 (1964)

IV

PETER MARCUSE

Groups concerned with open occupancy in housing sometimes find themselves perplexed by questions they had not anticipated. Take the experience of OURS (Open Urban Regions Society), a private group dedicated to the theory and practice of open occupancy in a typical Northern community, "Staid City." OURS starts off by regarding its job as educational; it holds meetings and distributes literature and arranges radio programs, and if it is very successful it gets some local television time, all to spread the fact to the white community that neighborhoods do not deteriorate when Negroes move in, to exhort

Peter Marcuse, who has written widely on housing quotas, practices law in Waterbury, Connecticut.

that democracy should be practiced in our home neighborhoods as well as overseas, et cetera.

It soon becomes apparent to OURS that all of this education is not really making much of a dent in the segregated pattern of housing in Staid City, and a new approach is developed. The state already has an open occupancy law, and OURS decides that what is really required is the vigorous enforcement of the law and a program to encourage its use. Again publicity, leaflets, radio, television, and meetings are turned to, but this time with their emphasis on a different audience: the Negroes who are living in the Staid City ghetto areas. As a result of much hard work, a number of complaints are actually filed with the State Civil Right Commission. Many of them turn out to be based on inadequate usable facts; in others the complainant either loses interest or finds housing elsewhere; in still others the landlord finally concedes but the tenant is unavailable for some other reason; and in some cases where the facts seem unusually propitious, the Commission finds one reason or another against pushing the case to a hearing. A few cases are successfully fought through and won, a few landlords back down, and over a period of several years OURS can point to several significant victories. At its annual meeting, however, a visiting expert gives some statistics on the extent of the growth of ghettos in the average Northern city, and the membership of OURS realizes that it is fighting a tidal wave with a whisk broom.

With dogged determination, OURS now turns its attention directly to helping Negro families find accommodations in segregated white neighborhoods. Education and publicity will no longer do; direct action is necessary. Proceeding in a businesslike fashion, OURS interests several foundations in providing funds, and sets up a program to provide on-the-spot assistance to Negro families looking for better places to live. Real estate licensing laws are carefully considered, a small office is located, a staff is hired, advertising is placed. A small problem is encountered in the wording of the advertisement—should it be addressed only to Negroes looking for homes, and should it say that it is looking for homes to be listed in white neighborhoods for sale to Negroes? The problem is not too difficult to solve; after some hesitation, the phrase "home owners willing to sell or rent to anyone regardless of race, creed, or color" is used, and ads looking for prospective home seekers are phrased to attract those "encountering discrimination in seeking a home." The program is moderately successful: Negroes do come in looking for homes, homes are listed, and on a number of occasions a buyer or tenant is happily matched with a seller or landlord.

To expand the scope of the program, the office is moved nearer the Negro community; to prevent it from being located so as to discourage sympathetic white visitors, it is established on the fringe rather than in the center of the Negro ghetto. Some additional prospective home owners and tenants are found in this way. Every now and then, a white man or woman comes in seeking assistance, and after some friendly conversation and advice, he is turned away. If he persists in asking about listings, the purpose of the organization is explained to him, and he is advised that only Negroes are being served by it. The average white reaction to this is not very positive, and occasionally a rather unpleasant scene takes place when a woman, usually the mother of several children and often a first-generation American, protests bitterly that her present housing is at least as bad as that of most Negroes and that the organization is discriminating against her, no matter what pious platitudes it may use to explain its position, but this is the exception rather than the rule.

If OURS is unusually daring, it will consider as a possible major expansion of its endeavors the attempt to have some branch of government actually take over its whole program. Reasoning quite logically that the problem is an over-all social one, of such scope that no private organization can really hope to make more than a small dent in it, OURS may well conclude that the Staid City government should establish a separate Housing Bureau whose purpose should be very specifically and openly the breaking down of the barriers of segregation and the placing of Negroes in decent homes in open neighborhoods. There may be some debate among the more sophisticated members of the group as to the desirability of imposing integration per se as a value upon some members of a minority group that do not particularly desire it; the practical realities will soon indicate to the group that the effort to help Negroes obtain better housing is almost invariably the same as the effort to break down racial barriers in predominantly white areas. The much more serious problem that will present itself to the group will be how to answer the accusation of members of the local legislative body, confronted with the proposal, who argue that this is class legislation favoring Negroes; that the needs of whites are just as great as those of Negroes; and that, if any critical social problem does exist in the area of housing, it should be faced and solved without regard for the individual's race, creed, or color; the facilities of the program should be available to all. The needs of the white family with five children living in a rat-infested slum are as great as the needs of a similar Negro family, the argument will run, and discrimination against that white family is as unjustified as discrimination against the Negro family would be. A program to improve housing, the hostile city fathers will say, has no excuse for recognizing color. When the OURS member tries to argue that establishing a program aimed at assisting Negroes in preference to whites is justified both by the moral obligation to make up to Negroes for the discrimination they have suffered in the past, and by the social desirability of integrated neighborhoods, even the friendly but sophisticated legislator will point out in reply that the open recognition of race and the passage of legislation consciously favoring one race over another will do more to harm the peaceful and harmonious relationships existing among various groups in Staid City than any good it might possibly accomplish. The apparently overwhelming public disfavor, echoed in newspaper editorials and letters to the editor, as well as statements at civic meetings, seems to bear out this contention.

Frustrated in their efforts to have Staid City establish a Housing Bureau to aid Negroes directly, OURS may well decide it must go into the housing construction business itself. As in most cities, there is an absolute shortage of decent housing, and the various groups within the city must compete for what is available. The over-all answer, OURS may decide, is to expand the total available supply of housing. Working in consultation with one of the experienced developers of open occupancy housing, OURS may raise the money and develop the organization to put up its own private development, and may embark on an aggressive sales program to show that open occupancy in new developments will work. The first two or three homes may be quickly purchased, and the leadership of OURS may be well pleased at the ease with which the sales were made; the next three and the three after that will likewise be relatively easy. One morning, however, OURS may awake to find that the first fifteen homes have all been sold to Negroes, and that as yet the only white living in the development is one of the board members of OURS. It will review the pending applications, and again find that substantially all are from Negroes. After some research and investigation of experiences in other communities, the phenomenon of the "tipping point," about which their consultants have warned them, will become evident to OURS: that whites will not easily move into a predominantly Negro area; that a certain percentage of Negro occupancy indicates to a large number of whites that the neighborhood will be predominantly Negro; and that the only way to keep a new housing development really integrated, given the tremendous pent-up demand among Negroes for homes, is to limit the number of Negroes so as to attract whites. OURS will try a number of techniques to attract more whites: they will cease advertising in Negro areas and concentrate on white-oriented publicity; they will ask the cooperation of the state and city Negro leadership in discouraging further Negro applicants; they will put pressure on those white applicants that showed some interest and discourage in sales techniques those Negroes on the waiting list; but they will find that none of these techniques are sufficient to really reverse the trend toward a new Negro ghetto. They will thus finally come to the paradox that in order to maintain truly open occupancy for Negroes and whites a quota must be put on the percentage of Negroes permitted to buy.

And thus, OURS will be faced with the supreme irony: first they have been accused of racial discrimination against whites, and now their dedicated group will find itself voluntarily discriminating against Negroes themselves because of their race! A more painful or more frustrating situation would be hard to imagine.

Perhaps OURS will decide that it should not itself venture into expanding the housing supply, but rather urge the Federal Government to assume its real responsibility in the area of low-income housing. Again, the same questions will intrude themselves on the beleaguered social conscience of OURS; the maintenance of integrated occupancy requires the making of decisions as to location, size, facilities, and architecture, as well as occupancy, based purely on race, and Federal officials will show more than the usual reluctance to admit publicly that any decisions should be made on such a basis. The legal problems arising from the overt consideration of race in order to avoid discrimination and segregation under fair housing laws—which, on their face, prohibit such consideration —are even more difficult in the Federal field, where pressures of nation-wide policy and publicity overlap with statutory and constitutional requirements. All in all, the members of OURS may easily feel that achieving real equality for all, regardless of race, creed, or color, involves solving problems much more difficult than the simple questions that first appeared on the surface.

The Arguments

The moral fervor with which the demand for preferential treatment is opposed by many who consider themselves loyal friends of the Negro is striking. Preferential treatment is discrimination in reverse, they say; it is no more proper for a Negro to ask for favored treatment over whites than it is for whites to receive favored treatment over Negroes. Justice demands equality without regard to color, and special treatment for Negroes means recognizing color just when the forward movement of history is turning toward obliteration of color as a factor in more and more areas of life. The Negro is not different from other minorities; why should he demand something no other minority has ever asked for, much less received? Certainly no white person can be asked to rally to a slogan that asks for favored treatment for the Negro, and at the expense of the white! Hypocrisy, selfishness, ignorance of history, and immorality, as well as a glaring mistake in tactics and strategy, are among the extreme labels given to the demand for preferential treatment for Negroes.

Compensation for past injustice, rather than undue advantage, is the simple phrase that many Negroes use to explain this new demand for different treatment. A race between a man brought up crippled and a man in full health is not made equal by avoiding further crippling; the proper solution is to give a handicap to the healthy, or a head start to the cripple. Recognition of color to remove inequality is a quite different thing from using it to impose servitude; there is no hypocrisy in wanting real equality as well as paper equality. The Negro's situation in America is one that has never been confronted by any other minority before, and the solutions to its problems must likewise be unique.

These are the most popular arguments on both sides of the hotly debated question of preferential treatment in liberal and civil rights circles today. The very term used to describe the special treatment being requested is loaded: "preferential treatment" implies giving undue advantages, whereas "compensatory treatment" carries with it the connotation of remedial action to right a wrong already committed. Since one or the other phrase has to be used from the beginning in discussing the problem, the reader may guess at this author's own ultimate conclusion by the use of the phrase "compensatory treatment" from here on in.

One of the more interesting features of the discussion of compensatory treatment is the moral vehemence with which the argument is often stated. Arguments about equality are seldom entirely free from emotion, but it is noteworthy that the civil rights sympathizer puts as much heat and energy into arguing against his friends when they ask for special treatment as he does into arguing for them when they do not. It is almost as if such persons were glad of the opportunity to separate themselves from the "extremists" in the Negro community. The attempt will be made here to discuss the pros and cons of compensatory treatment and to come to a conclusion based solely on logic and a careful analysis of the reasoning involved on both sides; nevertheless, there is usually a connection between the form in which an argument is presented and its content, and later on it will perhaps become clear why the argument against compensatory treatment is so often a heated one.

The question is not only whether to prefer or not to prefer; if there is an affirmative answer, a whole host of other questions arise. If preference is desirable, who is it that should do the preferring? Should it be compulsory for everyone, or for some, or should it be entirely voluntary? Should it be required by law, can it be regulated by law, or, indeed, is it even permissible under many existing laws? If the purpose of preference is compensation, when have we reached the point where enough has been paid? And who should do the paying—only those who were guilty of discrimination in the past, or everyone, regardless of his individual deserts? These are all questions that are just starting to be discussed, but they are questions that must be faced, and faced now; it is hoped the present discussion will contribute something to clarity in their answer.

Compensation and Need

In compensatory treatment, what is the compensation for? The question is hardly worth asking; it is compensation for three centuries of enslavement and mistreatment, for segregation and discrimination, for second-class status in almost all areas of life. But can "compensation" in this sense ever be made? Can we more than symbolically compensate for the thousands of slaves killed in the holds of the prison ships from Africa, for the families broken and the spirits maimed, for the physical beatings and deprivations of past generations? In a religious sense, perhaps atonement, rather than compensation, is possible, and the moral aspect of the problem is discussed very briefly below; in a legal or social sense, reparation can never be made for such injuries.

True compensation can be only the provision of present remedies for the present results of these injuries. Such provision is not directly geared to the amount of past deprivation, but rather to the amount of present need. George Washington Carver may have been the son of an uneducated slave, but his extraordinary inner resources were sufficient to overcome the almost insuperable obstacles placed in the paths of his achievement; on the other hand, even the child of a prosperous Negro small businessman today growing up in the ghetto of a large city and meeting the daily indignity of inferior status, may need extraordinary attention and help to grow up a healthy and well-educated human being, and even then he may find himself without a job or a decent home unless some further measures are taken. The need is created by past experiences which he, and his ancestors for many generations, suffered because of color; but the compensatory treatment is directed at his present need, not simply at his color.

Can preference because of color then be equated with preference because of need? For instance, if schools this child attends in the heart of the Negro ghetto require extensive special services, remedial programs, additional personnel and facilities, can the program be called one of assistance to schools in educationally deprived areas, or underprivileged areas, or areas of low socioeconomic characteristics, just as easily as it can be called a program of assistance to schools in the Negro ghetto? The result is certainly the same either way, and many people are considerably more comfortable with one formulation than with the other. Why not set aside all discussion of preferential treatment or compensatory treatment for Negroes and speak only of special assistance based on need? Everyone will realize, in this way, that prejudice for or against any color is not really involved, and, if one group happens to need help more than another, this is simply the result of historical and social circumstances, not an arbitrary desire to favor one group or another.

Disposing of the entire problem in this way is appealing, and as a practical matter there is no reason why it should not be done wherever possible. Regardless of their position on compensatory treatment in theory, most whites and, for other reasons, many Negroes, are reluctant to speak publicly of preferential treatment for Negroes. It runs against the grain to ask that a person be hired or assigned to a special class or given priority on a waiting list just because he is a Negro; and if there is some other phrase, be it euphemism or not, by which the same result can be accomplished, why not use it?

Need cannot be absolutely equated with color for several reasons. First, pragmatically, if reliance on "need" as the index for compensatory treatment precludes any frank use of color as a factor, the accomplishments are going to be much fewer and much slower in coming. Elaborate machinery will have to be set up in many cases to determine "need"; factors that are clearly statistically relevant will have to be ignored; red tape and social-workism will be tremendously increased. Looking at color happens to be quite an accurate short cut to identifying need, and avoiding its use makes such identification more difficult. The advantages of ignoring color may be considerable, but the disadvantages are also very real.

The second reason "need" cannot replace "color" entirely is that no matter what present status the Negro as an individual has been able to achieve, *every* Negro has suffered and been set back by the effects of past and present discrimination against Negroes as a group. Color itself, per se and not associated with any other economic or social or intellectual characteristic, has been a disadvantage in our society. Discrimination based on color alone has created needs that deserve to be met. George Washington Carver may have been able to make a significant contribution to America, but he nevertheless sustained injuries from discrimination and unfair treatment as great as—if with different results from—the unemployed factory worker or the impoverished sharecropper. If full justice is really sought after, it is not enough to aid the Negro at the bottom of the ladder; the professional Negro, the Negro businessman, and those able to climb the ladder despite their handicaps would each be much further along than they are if it were not for the immoral practices of a white society; their demand for compensation has an equally just and moral basis, despite a lesser objective need.

The Negro at the bottom of the economic ladder has an equal right to object to preference based solely on objective need. In terms of need, there will be white workers

as unskilled as he is, white youths as badly in need of a
job as he, white children as badly in need of remedial
education as his. Each of these individuals has needs based
on his unique personal experiences; but, in addition, each
individual Negro shares in a collective disadvantage suffered by all Negroes, and suffered by them solely because
of their color. An unskilled white worker and an unskilled
Negro worker may each be earning $60 a week, and thus
have equal objective needs; since the pattern of our society
has been to pay the Negro less for the same work, however, the Negro may actually be performing work worth
$80 a week, and, although his need is the same, his claim
to promotion and higher pay is clearly greater.

A sophisticated definition of need may still reconcile
these two areas of deviation between the standard of color
and the standard of need. Need can be measured by the
difference between what an individual has and what an individual requires to achieve those levels which society
recognizes as the minimums acceptable under current
standards. Need can also be measured by the difference
between what an individual has or what he is, and what
an individual should have to be that which he is capable of
being. In other words, we can measure need by the difference between the actual and the socially established
minimum, or we can measure it by the difference between
the actual and the potential. If we use the latter definition,
our $60-a-week Negro worker in all likelihood has a
greater need than his $60-a-week white brother, and the
color and the need of the Negro run a true parallel.

If it were possible to find a Negro in the United States who has never, directly or indirectly, been adversely affected by discrimination as it has been practiced for generations, all would probably agree that he should not receive preferential treatment; under this definition of need his exclusion from preference is clearly explained. Such a concept of need is not very useful in meeting day-to-day problems; it does, however, provide a theoretical underpinning for the discussion of the concept of compensatory treatment which follows.

Ethical and moral considerations may disturb this new parallelism between potential need and color. If, practically, reparation for past discrimination can never be fully made, is not compensation required for moral reasons? Is it not morally just that members of a group who in the past have been unjustly deprived be given compensating advantages to make up for these past injustices, even if such compensation would now put them ahead of where they may have been had neither the injustice nor the compensation taken place? In the terms of lawsuits for injuries suffered in automobile accidents, is not "pain and suffering" endured in the past worth some present payment? For most persons the answer to these questions will be yes, but the nature and extent of compensation based on these considerations must, almost by definition, vary with the individual answering and be incapable of exact measurement. From whom the compensation should come, whether individual "guilt" should be measured, or whether society as a whole should assume the burden—

these again will receive different answers from different ethical points of view. While the author recognizes the existence of these purely ethical or moral considerations, their treatment is outside the scope of this paper.

Two further complex problems, the value of integration per se in education, and the use of benign quotas in housing, play a role in the interconnection of need with color. In developing an educational program to overcome the ill effects of discrimination and segregation, an integrated classroom and school situation is of value as such, totally without reference to the respective needs for special attention or remedial effort of Negro or white children. The experience of integration itself, the creation of a democratic rather than a segregated environment, is required. Personal experience *with* the meaning of democracy and equality is necessary if the abstract teaching *about* them in the classroom is not to be negated by what the child sees when he looks about him; this is as important to the white child as it is to the Negro, and color in itself is a specific factor in the situation.

With benign quotas in housing, as previously illustrated, the problem is created by the existence of a tipping point, a Negro-to-white occupancy ratio at which, under present circumstances, a prospective white purchaser of a home or tenant of an apartment will feel that the percentage of Negro occupancy is so high that he will decide not to move in. This is a psychological phenomenon, based on the continued existence of prejudice and fear on the part of many whites; the establishment of benign quotas is to some extent a concession to such prejudices. Failure to recognize this problem may result in the further creation of all-Negro ghettos in new housing developments, and this author has elsewhere argued that the use of voluntary benign quotas, the attempt to obtain the voluntary cooperation of Negro applicants in maintaining an integrated occupancy, is the most desirable of several unsatisfactory solutions. In such situations, color pure and simple is the basis for determining the admissibility of an individual, with no reference to individual or group need at all.

The relationship of color to need is thus like the relationship of the red stripe to the white stripe on the barber pole. Going from the bottom to the top in a straight line, we may start with the idea of treatment according to need; next comes color as a rough index of need; this leads to deprivations resulting from color but not appearing as simple objective need; this in turn brings us back to an attempt to measure real need in some more sophisticated fashion; and this in turn leads us back to color. So the lines of color and need are parallel, but which follows which depends on where one stands and what point one is looking at. The line of color is perhaps more noticeable because of ethical factors, and problems of integration per se as a desirable result blur the lines a little. The logician will start with need, the picket captain with color; the adept polemicist will undoubtedly stress the interconnection. The fundamental importance of this interconnection will underlie the entire argument from this point on. We shall take for granted a high degree of congruence between color and need, unless otherwise noted.

The Case for Compensation

Louis Lomax makes the point, obvious once it is stated, that a major advantage of using Negroes as slaves rather than using indentured servants from parts of Europe is that Negroes could not escape and fade into the population without a trace. The Negro's visibility as a minority is much greater than that of any European immigrant group in the United States, and discrimination is therefore much easier to institute and continue against him than it is against others. The argument that other oppressed minority or immigrant groups have overcome similar problems without resorting to preferential or compensatory treatment is therefore from its inception a questionable one.

The early discovery that the Negro was an easily recognizable subject for discrimination was, at the beginning, a major factor leading toward the enslavement of a majority of Negroes; the extent of that enslavement, in turn, separated the Negro further from his society than any other minority group had ever been in America. At one point the quantitative difference between the extent of discrimination suffered by the Negro and that suffered by the Irish or other minority groups begins to mean that the character of the discrimination is also different. It is not oversimplifying to say that all other minority groups were at least granted a place, if only by default, at the bottom of the established society, whereas Negroes were kept entirely off the ladder and thus out of the society. Certainly the extreme racists in America are generally anti-Semitic and anti-Catholic as well as anti-Negro, but Jews and Catholics are still on the white side of the line, and Negroes are not. That line is harder and faster and more difficult to cross than any other ethnic, religious, or social line ever has been in this country.

The more sophisticated version of the argument about the Irishman and the Negro is what might be called the "waves" theory. This is that the Negro is only the most recent of a wave of immigrants of different ethnic backgrounds to come to this country, meet discrimination, and, after trials and tribulations of varying length, overcome it, only to see a new wave of immigrants come and go through the same process in turn. The only trouble with this view is that the Negro is not the most recent in a wave of minority groups suffering from discrimination. His was the very first (or, if the Indian's was the first, his was the second) group discriminated against in the United States, and it is still, three hundred years later, the one group most discriminated against. The Irish, the Italians, the Jews, the Eastern Europeans, and the Chinese have all come to this country at a time when the Negro was at the bottom of the economic spectrum; they have suffered discrimination, fought against it, by and large overcome it and themselves moved on up the ladder; and have seen a further minority group behind them go through the same process. But the Negro has been kept at the same position at the bottom of the heap as he was when they came. There is good likelihood that the same pattern will repeat itself both with the Mexican Americans and with Puerto Ricans, although this is by no means yet clear. In any event, such analogies between these groups and the Negro are not valid. It does not follow from the fact that the Negro's problems are qualitatively different from those that the Irishman faced, that the Negro should get compensatory treatment where the Irishman did not; but it equally does not follow from the fact that the Irishman did not need compensatory treatment that the Negro does not now need it. A brief look at the situation actually confronting the Negro will help answer the basic question.

The elimination of discrimination is of course the first order of business, and there is still a tremendous amount to be done in that direction. However, the long chain of historical discrimination against the Negro has created a situation which cannot be remedied simply by elimination of discrimination. In Mississippi, years of struggle may achieve court decisions guaranteeing equally administered voter registration tests; if Mississippi's educational system has kept many Negroes illiterate, permitting them to take these tests will not make them eligible to vote. Negro workers have for generations been denied the opportunity to acquire technical skills; opening up the skilled trades to all technically eligible applicants will not permit them now to become skilled workers. If the parents of a Negro youngster in New York were brought up in Mississippi, and if their outlook for the future and their view of themselves and the potential for their children is based on what they were taught in Mississippi, that youngster will need more than the same spelling class provided for a middle-class white youngster if he is to learn to read and write to the full extent of his abilities. The analogy of the free runner and the crippled or load-bearing runner has already been made here and elsewhere; without some additional help, the members of the group that has been kept back for generations will never catch up with their peers. This is the reasoning behind the campaign for compensatory treatment.

Compensatory treatment is part of the program for immediate and full equality, for a total end to discrimination now. Whites, as well as Negroes, will be the ultimate beneficiaries of such a policy. Discrimination, and the prejudice on which it is based, seriously distorts the perspective and the understanding of the person practicing it. Shadows are taken as substance, scapegoats for causes, prejudice against for superiority to. Democracy limited in one direction becomes susceptible to limitation in other directions as well. Children see that what is taught in school is not what exists in real life, and that some people are more equal than others. Freedom denied one group becomes restricted for all other groups as well. And of course society as a whole loses the full contribution of a major section of its people; effort and resources are poured instead in increasing quantity into the dike erected to protect from the pressure of all history the myth that one race is superior to the other. The time should be past when it is necessary to argue these points at length; if compensatory treatment helps to eliminate discrimination and prejudice and their effects, it is of benefit to Negro and white alike.

Problems of Law and Theory

Matters of principle are frequently argued out as legal questions in the United States. Perhaps this is because of the important role the written Constitution plays in our public life, and the concept of judicial review that has grown out of it; perhaps it is only because the reference to principles of law and court decisions provides a useful structure in which the argument can take place. In any event, the temptation to discuss compensatory treatment in terms of whether it is legally permissible, or consistent with the Constitution, is great. It is thus not surprising that a good part of the debate over the issue thus far has been in legal periodicals, and that the courts are responsible for more governmental pronouncements relevant to compensatory treatment than either the executive or the legislative branches of the government.

Legal arguments, however, cannot be permitted to determine fundamental political principles in a democracy. Laws are made by men, and, whatever the procedural roadblocks, they can be changed by men, and should be changed if they prevent the doing of what society conceives to be fundamental justice. Our discussion of the legal problems involved is therefore not intended to determine whether preferential treatment is legal or illegal under present laws and decisions, but only to see whether the legal formulations of the problem to date shed light on the social desirability of the policies under review.

The legal doctrine most often invoked in this area is that our system of government and law requires that the law be "color-blind." The phrase is of course taken from Justice Harlan's famous dissent in *Plessy* v. *Ferguson*. It has now been rebutted eloquently and at length in a number of popular as well as scholarly articles. One of the latest and best of these is Richard Lichtman's article in *Law in Transition Quarterly*. Essentially, the argument to the contrary is as follows:

The context of Justice Harlan's remark was that the law could not discriminate *against* any individual because of his color. Where color is directly relevant to a valid governmental purpose, however, it can be considered as much as age, sex, income, education, or any other relevant criteria. The extreme case, of course, is the one recently postulated to a class in constitutional law: the municipal ordinance requiring anyone with a black face to wear a white hat when walking along a dark highway at night. To take a more conventional example, a court reviewing the findings of a Fair Employment Practices Commission concerning discrimination against complainant A because of his color, must certainly inquire as to what A's color is before it can render its decision. Legislation shortly after the Civil War providing special benefits for freed slaves was really legislation assisting Negroes exclusively, and was deliberately designed to be such. Our philosophy would not tolerate discrimination against anyone because of his age; yet we award social security benefits only to those over sixty-two and do not hesitate to ask for birth certificates in determining eligibility. "Age blindness" should no more prevent this than "color blindness" should prevent assistance to those whose color puts them in particular need of such assistance.

As Lichtman says:

If the law cannot tolerate inequality is it not obligated to make men equal? . . . That the Negro ought to be treated equally is beyond question; that he is now effectively equal, is the denial of sanity. To treat him now as he ought to be treated in some ideal world—as though his color were irrelevant—this is not color blindness, but final moral obtuseness. . . . It would be the most terrible historical irony to misunderstand Mr. Justice Harlan's dissent as prohibiting support for the Negro, when that was the very passion of his outrage at the Court.

There is a reluctance among civil rights proponents to talk about assistance based on color because there is such a long history of the use of color for purposes of discrimination against Negroes, not help for them. Were it not for this, there would probably be little hesitation in saying frankly that there should be greater educational expenditures per pupil in areas of high Negro concentration than

in other areas, or in saying that special opportunities for
training and promotion should be made available to Negro
workers or job applicants. There is nothing in our Constitution, our legal tradition, or our philosophy that pre-
vents us from openly admitting that we desire to benefit
those who need assistance because of their color, where
this is the fact.

"Discrimination in reverse" is another phrase often used
to oppose compensatory treatment for Negroes in the
foregoing situations. The phrase presumably refers to
the fact that the policy advocated is one that is the reverse
of discrimination against Negroes, i.e., it is discrimination
for Negroes, and suffers in the same way from the vice
of action based on color. It thus means the same thing
as adherence to color blindness, and the answer is the
same: There is all the difference in the world between
harming someone because of an irrelevant characteristic,
and helping someone because of a relevant characteristic,
even though the characteristic be the same in both instances. It does not follow, from the fact that Negroes
should not be denied an education because of their color,
that, once they have been thus denied, we should not
recognize that Negroes are the ones who have in fact been
denied, and therefore are specially in need of remedial
assistance today.

Talk about color blindness does not answer the questions raised by compensatory treatment. Color blindness
was intended to protect Negroes from hostile discrimination, not to prevent efforts to overcome such discrimi-

nation and its effects. It is well accepted that he who has been discriminated against unfairly deserves to be made whole against the losses he has sustained because of such discrimination. To do this, the basis of the discrimination must be recognized. This is sufficient answer to the argument that the doctrine of color blindness precludes compensatory treatment of Negroes.

The "freedom of the individual" is the second legal doctrine often invoked in the dispute about compensatory treatment. Freedom is a many-splendored thing. Under its banner, slaves may justifiably revolt and nations throw off the bondage of foreign dominion. In its name, also, nations may attack smaller nations without provocation to protect the freedom of their own people, and, under its legal umbrella, freedom to contract can give one man control of the life and destiny of another. Freedom can mean freedom from discrimination and freedom to discriminate. It has been argued that any type of governmental action preventing discrimination, or, worse yet, any type of governmental action requiring or granting preferential treatment, violates the basic freedom of the individual to employ or not to employ, to house or not to house. Real estate boards and their friends, for instance, have been very prone to use the idea of freedom to protest against government regulation of or interference with their usual ways of doing business.

The negative end of this argument has been often rebutted. The right to hire whom one chooses is no more absolute than the right to drive as one chooses; limits reasonably related to the general welfare may be placed on each. The elimination of discrimination is reasonably related to the general welfare, and opinion is virtually unanimous that Fair Employment Practices acts are consonant with the fundamental principles of our Constitution. Exactly the same reasoning applies in the field of housing and, upon close analysis of the cases, the only serious constitutional disputes still involved relate to the form and means of enforcement of fair housing practices laws which are now already on the books in a number of states. Compensatory treatment, if otherwise desirable, should be equally permitted. Imposing an obligation to prefer one group of persons over another has been a not-unusual means of handling the problem of returning veterans, and the special aid given those physically handicapped by various employment services and school departments has never been seriously challenged as a violation of the principles of freedom.

Constitutionality does not always mean desirability; resolving the legal issue does not resolve the more basic question of policy. If the language of the Constitution does not preclude compensatory treatment, is it consistent with its spirit in a positive sense?

Our Constitution, by and large, is concerned only with political problems: the structure of government, the manner of its selection and the means for its change, restrictions on its power to regulate the broadly political liberties of its citizens, the separation of powers within it to prevent political abuses, and over-all limitations on its authority. One hundred seventy-five years of history have shown that it is flexible enough to permit a tremendous expansion of the powers of government beyond the areas originally contemplated; but the freedoms and rights it considered fundamental remain political ones. Political discrimination of any sort whatsoever is well on its way to being banned, and the current of constitutional thought arguing that political rights are absolute is a growing one.

Political rights, absolute or otherwise, do not exist in a vacuum. The context in which they are exercised is often as decisive of their real value as the legal protection they are accorded. To take one of the simplest examples, the right to vote appears to be about as basic and absolute a political right as we have. To be meaningful, it must extend to primaries as well as to general elections; to registration as well as to voting; to freedom from private intimidation as well as freedom from public discrimination. Current arguments about reapportionment illustrate in even more striking fashion that simple political rights cannot exist without carrying with them a whole host of political requirements that must also be fulfilled, so that a guarantee of one meaningful political right ultimately leads to a guarantee of many and perhaps all political rights.

In Mississippi, meaningful political rights involve governmental guarantees of even further rights that are not traditionally considered to be political. The right to an education, for instance, is not one guaranteed by the Constitution; yet the right to vote may with some reason be made to depend upon a minimal level of literacy. If it is, the right of the illiterate to be taught to read must exist if his right to vote is to make any sense. Observers of the newly developed countries of Africa and Asia have pointed out that real democracy and free elections cannot take place in a country where the citizens are often starving, ill-clothed, and ill-housed. If this is true, rights to minimal levels of food, clothing, and housing must accompany rights to vote. If a citizen can be discharged from his job for the way in which he votes, or for activities directed at having others vote the same way, then his vote is of course not really free; but if he has no job to begin with, and his life is a constant struggle for the bare necessities of existence, or is completely dependent on the benefactions of outside powers, his ability to cast an independent and intelligent vote is likewise practically nullified. His right to a job, therefore, has a direct bearing on the meaning of his right to vote.

The point need not be labored. Most of the political democracies that have been established in the twentieth century carry the theoretical recognition of these facts of life over their constitutional precepts, and include specific rights to food, clothing, housing, employment, and other "social welfare" types of benefits in their fundamental laws. Roosevelt's Four Freedoms included a recognition of the same forces; President Johnson's antipoverty campaign is perhaps the broadest recognition to date of the need to protect basic social and economic standards through governmental action in the United States.

Governmental protection of social and economic standards has obvious significance for the Negro. Census figures show the striking extent to which poverty, unemployment, slum housing, malnutrition, and below-subsistence-level incomes are concentrated among Negroes. A program aimed at remedying these conditions will be of particular benefit to Negroes, and Negro demands in these areas are increasingly insistent. If the political equality and formal freedom on which the United States prides itself are to be made real for all groups, these demands must be met; if the programs designed to meet such demands are of particular benefit for Negroes, it is not because of some unconstitutional preference for one group over another, but rather because of an entirely constitutional effort to meet needs that must be met where they exist most. The Constitution leads to rather than prohibits compensatory treatment.

Among the problems raised by compensatory treatment, few are as intriguing to the theoretician as the simple question of when to stop. Whether they are considered as moral atonement, elimination of social waste, or treatment based on needs, there is a point at which such measures will no longer be required by Negroes as a group. It may be that, in order to reach this point, it will first have to be overshot and then returned to; higher status in some areas may be needed to make up for deprivations in others. The real effects of centuries of second-class status may take decades to obliterate. However this may be, at some time such a point will be reached, and at that point compensatory treatment of any nature will no longer be required.

When the gap between real potential and actual performance, and between what is earned and what is paid, is the same for Negroes as for whites, presumably this exact point of relevant equality will have been reached. This is in theory an objectively measurable and provable point. Testing procedures have made real advances in recent years, and workers in that field are trying vigorously to develop techniques for measuring innate ability as compared to environmentally conditioned or acquired skills. In practice, it may be possible to verify most of the elements of such an evaluation in certain very limited areas, e.g., manual dexterity or mathematical performance. In many other areas, however, testing procedures are still rudimentary, and in still others the attempt has hardly been begun to develop objective tests to measure performance that is too complex and too closely related to social values to be identifiable and measurable. These would include such factors as political status, income, and creativity.

A rule of thumb that provides a very simple answer to the problem is the use of a quota. In employment this has obvious attraction. If the population of a community is 10 percent Negro, and the staff of a retail food chain within it is .2 percent Negro, the store is obviously discriminating; where its staff is 9 percent or 10 percent Negro, it is not. If $\frac{1}{15}$ of the workers in a plant are Negro, and $\frac{1}{15}$ of the foremen are Negro, there is probably no discrimination in filling the position of foreman. Likewise, in housing, if a private development is built in a community with a 3 percent Negro population, and 3 percent of it is occupied by Negroes, it is fairly representative of community patterns. In education, the same standards are applicable; if 28 percent of white students entering high school have dropped out by the end of their senior year, and the proportion of Negro dropouts is no higher, a basic success in overcoming the handicap of Negro students has been achieved.

The use of such quotas has obvious advantages: they are simple, easy to measure, easy to apply. Although the word "quotas" has bad connotations that go back many decades, sophisticated intergroup relations experts can accomplish much the same result that the use of quotas produces with pleasanter phrasing. An FEPC delegation, for instance, may find that an employer is discriminating against Negroes, and require him to remedy the practice. Its order will require regular reporting of the steps being taken to remedy past discrimination, that is, on the number of Negroes he is hiring. Periodically the Commission will confer with him to advise him of his progress according to their standards. If the Commission continues to find that, because his percentage of Negroes is below that in the community, the employer has not remedied his past discriminatory practices, yet urges him no further once the percentage reaches the community level, the Commission is really imposing a quota require-

ment, even though the word may never be used throughout the period of negotiation and enforcement.

But quotas have other implications also. Assume that
training as a machinist is required for further advancement as a tool and die maker, and that the percentage of
Negro tool and die makers is still far below what is considered desirable. If the hiring of Negro machinists were
ended when the "proper" percentage was reached, Negro
machinists would have a real right to object. The same
would be true of housing; a fair percentage of homes
occupied by Negroes in a $13,000 price range does not
mean that additional financial aid should not be afforded
those seeking homes in the $20,000 price range. Quotas
would have to be utilized for an entire category, not
merely any one section of it, and the definition of a category is by no means a simple one.

Jews today have a significantly greater proportion of
students in medical school than their numbers in the population at large would indicate; nevertheless, restrictions
imposed on the admission of more Jews are as burdensome
and degrading to the Jewish community as if the existing
proportions were lower. This is without any question of
compensatory treatment being desired. The particular
ability of any group, because of historical or social circumstances, in one area or one field of endeavor should
not be gainsaid because the requirements of equality have
been met on the average. When real equality has been
achieved, individuals should be judged on their own
merits, not by their membership in a group. If the social

sciences were exact sciences, and people were digits, perhaps quotas would be a satisfactory answer; as it is, they are not.

If we give up the effort to find a "perfect" answer about when to stop compensatory treatment, the problem is not so difficult. The concept of compensatory treatment is not welcomed by the Negro community itself as anything more than an unfortunate necessity. No man, woman, or child likes to be singled out as needing special assistance; every individual wants to stand on his own two feet, and compensatory treatment beyond a certain point is an affront to pride and an insult to dignity. Particularly is this so when race is involved, and each minor example of preference is a continual reminder of racial differentiation. The Negro community itself will therefore demand no more compensation than is required to permit it to overcome those handicaps that past discrimination has caused; past that point, the Negro community will be as vehemently opposed to preferential treatment as some members of the white community are now.

The problem of ending compensatory treatment once it is begun is really the problem of weighing the over-all social gain in the further elimination of the effects of discrimination against the over-all social losses resulting from continued differential treatment based on race. As compensatory treatment and other private and public action lead to greater actual equality, the weights on each side of the scale will change, and at one point the disadvantages will outweigh the advantages. Where that point is will be a political decision, and there is no reason why it cannot be solved by the normal political institutions of our government. Just as veterans have been given a preference, but a line has been slowly and often painfully worked out beyond which that preference does not extend, so will the limitations of "preferential" quotas slowly and perhaps painfully be worked out. In a democracy, the ultimate judge of the social desirability of a given course of action is the people themselves, acting through their government; they also will determine the point beyond which compensatory treatment is no longer required.

The quota question, like the related question of when to stop compensatory treatment, can be exaggerated beyond all proportion to its actual importance; in some cases such exaggeration may be done deliberately and maliciously. It is not of critical importance. When a company has for years discriminated against Negroes, it can be required to end its discriminatory practices and affirmatively attempt to hire Negroes, without its having at the same time to be told when it has hired enough. When no Negroes at all live in a given neighborhood, they can be encouraged to move in without any preconceived statement of how many there should ultimately be. Sometimes it is necessary to start even without knowing exactly on what day and at what number the end will come; compensatory treatment is such a situation. If all progress were to wait till its goals were established with mathematical certainty, there would be much less forward movement in the world.

Problems of Implementation

Deciding on the desirability of compensatory treatment is unfortunately only the beginning of the problem, not the end. The proper form for such a policy must still be determined, and then the means by which society can be persuaded to put it into effect. The simplest form for such a policy would be if every employer, every property owner, and every educator naturally and freely put the concept into practice. Unfortunately, life is not so simple. When the Pitney-Bowes Company in Stamford, Connecticut, announced a company policy of recruiting potentially qualified Negroes, its statement attracted national publicity; few, if any, large companies have followed in its footsteps. Announcement of a proposed housing development in Deerfield, Illinois, which would attract Negro as well as white families into that Chicago suburb was enough to unleash all the forces of community hostility to frustrate its developers' plans. The intelligent action of some progressive school districts in planning their school building programs, drawing their attendance lines, allocating special services, instructional material, and experienced teachers—all on the basis of the actual needs of the school population, thus favoring Negro children and Negro-attended schools—has drawn national attention and, in many cases, outspoken opposition. The number of districts actively seeking to solve these problems is still a tiny minority of those facing them.

If Pitney-Bowes were the only employer in the country, there would be no problem; it is, however, only one of thousands of employers that engage millions of employees in the United States. Granted, there will never be total uniformity or total fairness in all parts of this country at the same time in the same way. But giant steps can be taken so that the handling of this situation is as similar in one place as in another. This can only be done by the active intervention of government in making decisions on such questions of employment. If compensatory hiring is a desirable policy, it is desirable to have each individual employer act along the lines indicated. If it is desirable, it is not so because of any direct connection with the profit motive, but because of considerations based on broad social policy. These are traditionally the concern of government, rather than private industry, and only the government can make such policies nationally effective within any reasonable period of time.

Governmental intervention, at the Federal level, is also required to prevent obvious injustice to the more socially progressive employer, real estate operator, or educator. Compensatory treatment, by definition, is economically unwise from the individual employer's point of view. Perhaps it does not cost an employer more to hire a Negro in preference to a white when each is equally qualified; but when he hires a Negro less qualified, though still able to do the job, the employer loses in terms of efficiency and productivity. When he is asked to go still further and provide special training for the Negro employee to assure him of an equal opportunity for advancement, the additional cost is measurable, for it is the cost of that special training compared to the lesser or nonexistent cost of training the qualified white applicant for the same job.

In principle, it may not be unfair for an employer to pay out of his own pocket now to redress some of the wrongs from which he himself has benefited in the past. However, when one employer voluntarily assumes this burden, and others do not, he is putting himself at a competitive disadvantage. The injustice of penalizing the progressive employer is compounded by the fact that in all likelihood his particular firm was less involved in the prevailing patterns of discrimination than other more backward firms; yet his compensatory treatment helps the backward firm compete on more favorable terms with him.

The only fair answer to the dilemma is to spread the temporary economic burden equitably over the entire employer community. When the Federal Government bears the burden of the retraining program, the progressive employer is assisted; when it does so with funds raised by a progressive income tax, all employers are participating in paying for that burden. The same reasoning applies in each other field; the critical role of the Federal Government must be realized and acted upon before compensatory treatment can be either generally effective or generally equitable.

Certain steps pointing in the direction of long-term answers are already being taken in many areas. The Federal Government is adopting a policy of active Negro recruitment in a number of fields; when it does so in staffing a Dallas post office, the critical reactions are loud and clear; when it does so in staffing its Connecticut vocational retraining offices, it is quietly commended. Formal preference is not yet really being given in terms of actual hiring or promotion, but only in recruitment and encouragement; the principle involved is the same. In planning the location and the occupancy policies of public housing projects, sophisticated attention is now being given to the effect of varying decisions on racial patterns. And the U.S. Department of Health, Education and Welfare is giving increasing attention to the way in which Negro children can be aided in overcoming some of the detriments of their past deprivations.

The side effects of certain new Federal programs are even more interesting. The Manpower Development and Training Act has resulted in many instances in programs specifically benefiting those Negro unemployed and underemployed who are most in need of training and/or retraining. The programs of the President's Committee on Juvenile Delinquency have, in probably most instances, been concentrated in areas of heavy Negro population. The Economic Opportunity Act of 1964, the antipoverty program, will also inevitably be of unusual benefit to Negroes, who constitute a great deal more than their proportionate part of the "poverty population" of most communities. These programs witness the expansion of the Federal Government's intervention directly into areas which had previously been exclusively private preserves, or, at most, in which local or state governments had assumed minimum remedial rather than preventive roles. One example will show the difference between the old and the newer approach.

Few areas are usually considered more clearly private in nature than the hiring policies of private employers. In that minority of states which provide some real regulation of hiring, governmental intervention has in the past been purely negative: discrimination because of race, creed, or color is banned. This type of legislation is generally ineffective in remedying indirect discrimination; it cannot regulate the manner in which active recruitment for job openings is done, and it is totally ineffective in providing for overcoming the effects of past discrimination by open compensatory hiring or training. By taking statistical evidence of an abnormally low ratio of Negroes in the working force as informal evidence of discrimination, the most progressive civil rights enforcement agencies may be able to exert pressure on an employer to actually hire on a partially compensatory basis; as yet there are real limits beyond which such pressure cannot go. By and large, the effect of FEPC laws has been to prevent further discrimination, not to remedy past acts.

The new Federal legislation tackles the problem from a different angle. In effect it subsidizes the "preferential" training of those with the greatest handicap, and a realistically administered program will thus often specifically subsidize the training of Negroes. At the same time, employers are encouraged to hire those specifically trained to meet their job requirements. The compensatory hiring of Negroes is thus accomplished constructively—if through the back door. To the extent that need is equated with color, compensatory treatment enters the front door, and if the program proves a success, it may well be a permanent resident in the house. Hopefully, the expansion of the activities of the Federal Government in the housing field, currently moving forward erratically and at a snail's pace, will end up at the same place. The educational features of the antipoverty program will have to favor Negro children from the outset if they are truly based on need; specific technical assistance provided to school systems in the process of desegregating is provided for under the Civil Rights Act of 1964. It is no accident that, in a society which has become dramatically aware that one hundred years of inaction have not erased the aftereffects of slavery, attention is being sharply focused on the need for tremendously expanded action by the Federal Government to make up for lost time. Only constructive Federal action, in areas hitherto considered private, can solve these problems in less than another one hundred years.

Strategy and Tactics

Having decided that compensatory treatment is desirable, and what shape it should take, how are we to persuade the essential individuals and groups to put it into effect? The opposition to compensatory treatment is loud and strong. It comes not only from segregationists and conservatives but also from many in the white community who are favorable in theory to civil rights and the struggle for emancipation of the Negro. To learn the means to overcome the opposition, one must learn its causes.

Part of the explanation for the opposition lies in the loyalty to shibboleths whose meaning either has disappeared or is no longer relevant: the shibboleths of "color blindness," formal equality, and hostility to preference connected with color in any way. The irrelevance of these phrases has already been discussed: the argument is so bothersome precisely because these phrases have been symbols for which civil rights sympathizers have so long fought that to give them up is a difficult and sometimes painful process.

The widespread nature of the hostility to preferential treatment, however, goes deeper than a mere allegiance to outworn phrases. Emotions are involved because "bread and butter" issues are involved. The reaction is the cry that if one person or group receives a preference, it must be received at the expense of another person or group. If the group that is given the advantages of a preference is the Negro group, the group at whose expense it is given is the white group. No deep explanations are required to explain the hostility to preferential treatment for the Negro on the part of the insecure white who has come to this conclusion. Although the reasoning on which this reaction is based is not often expressed openly, since it makes opposition to preferential treatment look like a selfish thing, it undoubtedly underlies much of the reaction. Whether the critics of preferential treatment are ashamed in theory to make the argument or not, the communities in which the policy is put forward include many who feel this way, and the argument must be met and resolved if broad public acceptance is ever to be attained for the policy.

That the reasoning is superficially plausible is hard to deny. At its simplest level, if a company has to hire one individual, and a Negro and a white of equal qualifications apply, the white remains unemployed if the Negro is hired. If promotion to a better-paying job is involved, a white is deprived of money in his pocket if a Negro is chosen. If special training programs are established for Negroes, whites otherwise eligible will be deprived of that opportunity for advancement while Negroes move ahead at their expense.

In the educational field, self-interest also comes into play. Whether a new high school is all-white or half-Negro and half-white does not seem to affect the welfare of any unbiased white child particularly. A variety of factors may, however, have hindered the educational growth of the Negro child, and made him in many cases a more difficult child to teach, with less strong motivation and less outside stimulation than his white counterpart. Therefore, some white parents may feel that their chil-

dren will be pulled backward by the presence of a significant number of Negro children, from a purely educational
standpoint and without regard to color. Such parents, of
course, ignore the importance of a more democratic education, diversity of experience, and the manifold ways
in which the educational problems referred to can be
overcome; the point is only that there is a very direct
personal and selfish interest felt to be at stake. This un-
deniably explains a good bit of the white community's
hostility to many plans for integration of public education.

Actually, even the most innocuous-appearing program
for the redress of the wrongs imposed by discrimination
and segregation contains an element of preference for
Negroes at the expense of whites. When extra specialized
teachers, reading consultants, social workers, and other
special personnel are assigned to schools with heavy
Negro populations, they are that much less available to
the other schools. When a concentration of social services
or public services is arranged for in a Negro portion of a
community, the remainder of the community receives less.
If the demand of Negroes for housing is greater than that
of whites, so that the limited amount of public housing
available is occupied largely by Negroes, white applicants
may themselves feel discriminated against. In each of these
instances, there will be either a direct or an indirect hardship to a white person through action benefiting the Negro. Taken to its extremes, the argument, of course, applies

to virtually any activity that involves expenditure of public funds in the interest of protecting civil rights or benefiting those deprived of them; when a tax dollar is spent to
pay the salary of an employee of a Fair Employment Practices Commission, that tax dollar comes disproportionately
from the white community, and some are thus required
to pay out disproportionate tax money for the protection
of the civil rights of others.

The extreme example, of course, points out the basic
fallacy of the argument. Our whole political system has
long recognized that the welfare of one segment of society
cannot be separated from the welfare of another, and it is
taken for granted that all persons have a certain minimum
obligation to contribute to programs which may help
others more than themselves, the rationale being that such
programs contribute to the over-all progress and tran-
quillity of society. Exactly the same principle is involved
with compensatory treatment. The real integration of
Negroes into American life, the reduction of racial ten-
sions, and the freeing of the vast potentials that such action may achieve, are all of benefit to each person in
society, whether that person is Negro or white. The income of the president of General Motors is taxed at a
higher rate than the income of an assembly line worker in
one of his plants, and the money is used in part to pay
unemployment benefits to that worker if he is laid off; this
is accepted because it is recognized that the resultant advantage to society benefits the president of General

Motors and all other high-income taxpayers in sufficient degree to justify the disproportionate burden. The income tax was a hard pill for many to swallow, just as compensatory treatment will not easily be acceptable to many; the logic of both is exactly the same.

Logic has, of course, never been the decisive factor in resolving social disputes, and there is no reason to think the question of compensatory treatment is any exception. The income tax was made feasible in large part because our political system gives legally equal weight to the vote of the individual who is poor as well as the individual who is rich, and those advantaged by a progressive income tax significantly outnumbered those disadvantaged by it. This is not the situation with compensatory treatment. In most parts of the country, whites outnumber Negroes significantly, and unless the support of whites can be obtained for the proposed program, it will not go far. If no way can be found around the problem of an actual or supposed conflict of interests, compensatory treatment can probably be junked as a workable idea.

There is one policy by which the conflict can be mitigated, however. If the white displaced by the Negro in hiring *stays* unemployed, his reaction will be sharp and clear. If, instead of remaining unemployed, he is also employed, but perhaps at a job that is only his second preference, his reaction will be proportionately less hostile. If a training program is open only to Negroes, and a white worker is doomed to remain forever on an assembly line job, his feelings can be imagined; if a white worker has substantially similar opportunities for advancement, his antagonism will be much reduced. If reading consultants are taken from a white classroom and used in a Negro classroom, the parents of the white children may well be expected to object; if additional reading consultants are made available so that each child will have what he needs, much less objection will be encountered. In short, if the legitimate need of the Negro requiring compensatory treatment is honored, but at the same time the legitimate if slightly lesser need of the white is also taken care of, the clash becomes much less sharp, if it is not virtually eliminated.

The implications of this line of thinking are far-reaching and have already been acted upon in many areas by the leadership of the civil rights movement. What it means essentially is developing a coordinated program for the solution of the problems of those sections of the white community in need of assistance at the same time as programs for the aid of the Negro community are developed. On an organizational level, it means creating an alliance between the Negro civil rights movement and the organizations of the lower-income white community. It means tying the program for special assistance to Negro school students to an over-all school improvement program. It means tying the program for preferential hiring of Negroes into a program for increasing over-all employment. These connections have already been made in many areas, and they are essential to the adequate handling of the problem here discussed.

The strategy for winning compensatory treatment is not easy. The idea itself, as an abstract doctrine, requires some re-examination of conventional democratic catch-words and cliches. It has implications, as will be shown in the conclusion, that are far-reaching indeed. For any person or group not directly concerned with the problems that cause the need for compensatory treatment, either a real intellectual effort or some more dramatic over-all approach highlighting the real importance of the proposed policy is required. Neither is easy, and the particular circumstances must govern what approach is used.

In states which already have broad legislation against discrimination in the key areas of housing and employment, and so have already determined that segregation in education is educationally undesirable, the development of techniques of compensatory treatment may be the next order of business. Most states are not this far along, and here the campaign to obtain compensatory treatment may conflict with the campaign to first end discrimination.

Usually the first step leads to the second, but this is not necessarily true in the current situation. As we have analyzed it, a desire for true equality does, in fact, lead inevitably to the need for compensatory treatment to make up for past handicaps. But the first step uses the slogan of equality to defeat discrimination based on color; the second step requires discrimination based on color to achieve

fuller equality. Words get in the way, and form is confused with substance; compensatory treatment is not an
easy subject to discuss even in a symposium including
experts in the field, let alone in an election campaign in
a typical American town. The request for compensatory
treatment can be a real detriment to a drive for FEPC or
fair housing practices legislation. In such situations, the
importance of the first step may outweigh the need to
prepare for the second.

In other situations also it may be wiser to postpone a
general discussion of compensatory treatment. Certainly
any serious discussion of such treatment must acknowl-
edge that, by and large, the question is still a theoretical
one, and its resolution is far from the first order of business
in most cases. So long as deliberate or overt discrimination
exists, its elimination is the first problem. Such discrimination does still exist, in the North as well as in the South,
to a much greater degree than many people like to admit.
Under such circumstances, focusing undue attention on
the theoretical problems of preferential treatment may be
a disservice to the civil rights movement in two ways.
First, it may carry with it the implication that the elimination of discrimination has already been achieved, or is just
around the corner and can be achieved without much
more trouble—an implication very far from the truth
and potentially dangerously misleading. Second, it focuses
attention on a problem on which many in the Negro community and in the civil rights movement are as yet divided;
thus it highlights disagreements in a sensitive but remote

area, rather than emphasizing the unity that is often crucial in resolving day-to-day issues. The demand for compensatory treatment can become seriously distorted if not seen both in perspective and in context.

Conclusion

There is an unspoken assumption that has run throughout this discussion thus far. We began by pointing out that the mere end of discrimination was not enough to achieve actual equality for the Negro; we weighed the alternatives to compensatory treatment, and found them effective up to a point, but insufficient as a comprehensive answer; we were thus led to conclude that compensatory treatment was the only method of guaranteeing true equality. We then analyzed "compensatory treatment," and found that, in theory and apart from moral and certain other factors, it was the same thing as preference based on need. In practice, color nevertheless had to be relied on as an index of need in many situations, and the moral responsibility of our society for past discrimination made this doubly proper.

We then considered the constitutional status of compensatory treatment. We decided that the doctrine of "color blindness" was designed to prevent discrimination against any individual because of color, not to prevent its cure; and we decided that private freedom and due process of law were not unreasonably invaded by a requirement of compensatory treatment. Quite to the contrary, we pointed out the ways in which existing constitutional guarantees almost required compensatory action in certain circumstances.

We found that putting such a program into practice was ultimately possible only by relying on intensive Federal governmental action, and such action was also the only way of avoiding an unequal and unfair impact of the program on those few voluntarily putting it into effect. We then discussed the difficult strategy required for the implementation of a program of compensatory treatment; not only should such a program be prevented from interfering with the first priority of ending actual discrimination where it still exists, but the program should be linked with a broader program to increase the total available supply of jobs, homes, and educational services, so that the advantage of one would not result in the disadvantage of another similarly situated.

Somehow, in all our previous discussion, we have never directly confronted the question of the ultimate purpose of compensatory treatment. We started out by saying it was to meet those special needs created by past discrimination. Is its purpose then simply to achieve an absolute equality of status and opportunity between Negro and white, just as if there had never been any discrimination? If so, many of the slogans that are normally associated with campaigns for compensatory treatment are quite irrelevant. The goal is then not jobs and full employment, but only equal unemployment; not better housing, but an equitable distribution of both good and bad housing; not better education, but an equal statistical possibility of learning something or learning nothing in school. The pure logic of compensatory treatment does not lead beyond this point; where the present argument has gone beyond it, it has done so only in the tangential fields of strategy, where a broader campaign was recommended to make the policy acceptable, and in the field of law, where a different formulation, based on need, was suggested as substantially identical in substance but more acceptable in form.

The campaign for compensatory treatment is not, however, an isolated program existing in a vacuum. It has come about because of, and as an integral part of, the broad struggle for civil rights of the Negro in America. This struggle is not for an empty legal equality of rights; it is for meaningful, effective rights which will actually improve the living conditions of those obtaining them. While we speak of equality of opportunity as a goal in its own right, the force of history and circumstances has linked it inextricably with the goal of actual opportunity. Negroes and their allies are not just seeking equal housing, they are seeking decent housing; not just an equal opportunity to apply for or get a job, but a job there to be gotten; not just the same education as everyone else, but a sound and significant education, leading to a richer and freer life in a better society.

Compensatory treatment is but one part of the movement in this direction, and its development at each step of the way is connected with the logic of the movement as a whole. When the program for compensatory treatment leads to a strategy of demands for an absolute increase in the available supply of goods and services, what appears as strategy from one point of view becomes a matter of principle in the context of the movement as a whole. When Federal intervention seems the only logical way to make compensatory treatment either generally effective or socially fair, the movement as a whole sees it as part of a broad need for expansion of the Federal Government's role.

The underlying, unspoken assumption of our argument thus far has been that the problems compensatory treatment is designed to solve should be solved. The assumption seems hardly arguable, and basic ethical considerations are sufficient to support it. In addition, the social benefit from greater utilization of potential, the greater freedom and rationality resulting for both Negro and white, and similar arguments can be adduced. In the context of the broader historical movement, however, the campaign for compensatory treatment becomes one manifestation of a much more significant campaign: the campaign for the minimum requirements for *all* citizens to lead a full and rich life, the view that society as a whole has a responsibility to secure the conditions that lead to such a result. The meeting point of these two lines of development— civil rights for Negroes and betterment for all men—is the equation of color and need.

The turbulence caused by the juncture of these two currents also explains some of the passion generated by the argument over compensatory treatment. An effort to obtain equality of misery threatens few vested interests; where misery is widespread, and a preferred position in poverty over a Negro neighbor constitutes the sole lifeline to prestige, as in Mississippi, the Negro's simple request for equality evokes its strongest resistance. When the effort is not only to obtain equality but also to obtain the real opportunity to exercise it, then really conflicting economic, social, and political interests come into play. Public or publicly assisted housing, greater public expenditures on schools, guaranteed full employment, are all issues on which the cleavages in our society run deep; the current of civil rights sharpens them, although it does not cause them.

The logical and ethical questions raised by the demand for compensatory treatment are substantial and complex, and they require some sophisticated answers. The broader movement of which such a demand is but part raises even broader questions, and one set of questions cannot be resolved without the other. Does our society recognize an obligation to help its citizens lead a full and rewarding life, decently housed, adequately clothed and fed, educated to an appreciation of the wonders of the world in which they live, and able to partake of them? Or does our society see its role as guaranteeing only the legal prerequisites for these goals, protecting life and liberty and hoping these in turn will permit a successful pursuit of happiness?

Answers can be suggested for the questions involved in compensatory treatment by abstract logic and ethics alone; but the question of the importance of the idea and the role it will play can only be answered if these broader questions are also resolved.